"Red Dirt Revelations"

A Collection Of Memories From Vietnam Veterans

Copyright 2024, Chad Spawr

ISBN: 9798325180286 with Amazon/Kindle Books

Cover Design: Seajay Milner
Page Layout: Sam Milner
with
Sea Dunes Books
seadunesbooks@gmail.com

C. V. (Chad) Spawr
Vietnam Veteran 1967-1969

D1618143

Contents

Introduction

The word "revelation" in a non-religious context is generally defined as:

a. *An act of revealing in order to view or make known.*

b. *Something that is revealed, especially an enlightening or astonishing disclosure.*

While it may appear that the choice of the word "revelation" is designed to impart some great sense of truth or some mysterious purpose to the war in which we served, the reality is that virtually everything we experienced as soldiers, sailors, airmen, and Marines was "revelatory."

Before our service, none of us had ever been under enemy fire, never fired on another human being, never been confronted with the violent deaths of friends, had never dealt with the extreme environmental conditions such as monsoon rains, fetid rice paddies, "natural" environments populated with venomous snakes, foot-long centipedes, tigers, or water buffalo that would attack us because they didn't like our smell. These and other experiences were new to all of us, opening us to a range of emotions and fears that were with us not only for our tours of duty, but have been part of our lives ever after.

This book presents memories of several veterans of the Vietnam War. The memories are our own, not pre-selected nor chosen for the veteran. They are our memories of things that happened, and most were revelatory for the experience, but may also be revelatory for readers who have no idea of what life was like in a Southeast Asian war zone. For the most part, these memories are things we have seldom, if ever, shared with others, simply because nobody asked, or seemed to care. Almost every combat veteran from every war ever fought knows what that means.

3

We don't volunteer such memories, as we simply don't believe most people would understand them. Why spend time explaining something people either don't want to hear about or couldn't understand if we did? So, given all of that, why this book?

Much of the Southeast Asian landmass, including that of Vietnam, is composed of mountains, jungles, fruit plantations, rice paddies, and undeveloped areas growing out of an iron-rich soil known as "laterite,"  a soil that is deep red in color. Its dust and particulates collect and gather in every possible way in regard to human endeavor. When it is wet, it is an incredibly thick and heavy mud; when bone dry, it flies as if on wings, and can be blown hundreds of feet into the air by helicopter rotors, airplane propellers and jet engines. There is simply no way to avoid the "red menace." And…it will stay with you even for years after leaving Vietnam. Whatever else we had in common, we all lived in, breathed, swallowed some of that red dirt. It was ground into our skin, part of the waxy buildups in our ears, hardened like concrete under our fingernails.

My Dad was a World War II Veteran, but he would never talk about his experiences. In 1969, when I told Dad that I was being assigned to Fort Bragg, NC, he didn't tell me that he had been stationed at Bragg in World War II, and was part of the growing Army that developed Bragg from a remote artillery training base to a major training and deployment base. I learned this only after he had passed.

4

It was the same with my Dad's brother who served in the Navy during World War II, primarily in the Pacific Theater. He was a Torpedo-man on the Destroyer USS *William Porter*. His ship was sunk by a kamikaze attack off Okinawa where he was badly injured with a broken back. He obviously was rescued and recovered enough to complete a successful career as a Michigan State Police officer. However he never talked about "his" war, never mentioned he'd been wounded. In fact, I didn't learn of his broken back until nearly sixty years later when I was searching some WW-II records from the Okinawa battle. Those old guys just didn't talk about their wartime experiences! Who would have understood?

After the Vietnam War, this country made it clear it did not want to hear about Vietnam. The situation was compounded by a national media seemingly fixated on portraying the war as a horrible mistake and the soldiers fighting it worse than war criminals. I clearly remember a national network news story with a video clip of an American soldier lighting a thatched roof hut on fire, the media claiming we were deliberately destroying peasant houses. Never mind the fact that the "house" was an overhead cover for Viet Cong arms and food cache, and there were no civilians living in the area. The message was delivered by a politically compliant media.

On more than one occasion, several of us discussed writing a book to capture our stories. The idea was that we'd all contribute to the book and provide a "man in the street" approach by individual warriors so "our" story could be told honestly and fairly. For what it is worth, the idea never died with me. I thought about it in the intervening years but given demands on my time and energy from a growing family, working career, a return to graduate school and then back to work in senior management roles that required frequent international travel, it remained an idea only.

5

I met another Vietnam Veteran and we chatted about the possibility of such a book. Conversations with Tony Kay were productive, and you'll find his chapter included in this book. I had also discussed this project with Jeff Holst, a Navy Veteran who had fought in the Mekong Delta. His story is also included. Seems the concept had some traction after all.

This book is designed to honor its writers, to share some of our memories. It is not intended to be "literature" or teach any great lessons of history or morality. Rather than focusing on war and combat, the writers are telling their stories, memories, observations, and recollections of a time in their lives when the norm was totally abnormal.

Each of the contributors of this book experienced the Vietnam War directly through painful experience and even deep personal loss. For many, the war has continued for decades after we came home, and will end only when we take our DEROS to the sky.

If we've played our cards well, we'll never again see that red dirt!

Howard B. Patrick
Sergeant, Echo 1/5 Recon
2d Brigade 1st Cavalry Division (Airmobile) Civil Affairs Team
1968 – 1969

"Why Not Me?"

Why? By itself, the word *why* is normally used to question a previous statement or comment. When it precedes a specific topic, it is normally questioning something about that topic. But when followed by the single word *me,* it takes on a unique type of question, one that is often asking why a particular misfortune, such as a serious illness or personal hardship, befell the person. When followed by the words *not me*, that question is usually asked by those who believe, feel, or wonder why others were so fortunate, or lucky, and they were not. When I ask myself *why not me,* I am not questioning my lack of good fortune—just the opposite. I'm trying to find a reason why was my life was spared while others were not. Why did others die, when I, facing certain death, survived?

7

1967 started off great. I was a 23-year-old newlywed, a recent graduate of an Electronics Engineering Technology program from a local Philadelphia technical school, and two months into a new job as a computer technician with IBM, the most prominent computer company in the country. My life could not have been any better. But a few short months later, all that changed with the arrival of a letter that would thrust me into the most perilous time of my life.

I walked into our apartment after work, but instead of being greeted by my wife's smiling face and a lingering kiss, I found Judy sitting hunched over on the couch, sobbing nonstop, her eyes red and puffy, and her face drained of color. My immediate thought was that someone in the family must be seriously ill or injured, maybe even dead. Judy didn't say a word. Still sobbing, she just looked up, and with a trembling hand gave me the tear-stained letter she had been clutching. It was an induction notice from my local draft board, instructing me to report to the Philadelphia Military Induction Center on April 17. I had been drafted. And the first thing that popped into my mind was *why me?* No one I knew had gotten drafted, just me. Why none of my friends, why only me? There had been a deferment for married men, but that was revoked shortly before I got married. And since I was in perfect health, there didn't seem to be any way to avoid going. IBM was able to get me a one-month postponement, which pushed my reporting date back to May 15.

In spite of my technical training and experience, the army decided I could best serve my country in the infantry. I was offered Officer Candidate School, but turned it down because it meant an additional ten months of service. Following a year of training, including 22 weeks at NCO School, I was promoted to the rank of sergeant and given a reporting date to be in Oakland, California— next stop, Vietnam. However, an unexpected family health crisis resulted in a 30-day emergency leave that delayed my departure until ten days after the birth of my daughter. Upon arriving in Vietnam I was assigned to the First Cavalry Division as a squad leader with Echo Recon, (E Company, 1st Battalion, 5th Regiment), a newly formed reconnaissance company. Halfway through my tour I was transferred to the Brigade Civil Affairs Unit as the NCO-In-Charge, where I also participated in air missions with the attached Psychological Operations (PSYOPs) Group.

On paper, our prime objective was to conduct reconnaissance missions in suspected enemy areas to provide information about the enemy to our battalion. However, during Echo Recon's first year of operations our small recon unit had the highest kill ration of any unit in the First Cav in that same time period. We did have casualties, but there were only a handful of fatalities. As part of our normal ambush procedures we placed Claymore mines (directional, command-detonated anti-personnel mines) pointed outward from our position toward the trail we were hoping enemy soldiers would come down. When triggered, the Claymore sends a wide pattern of metal balls into the kill zone like a shotgun. On one of our night ambushes my squad set up a semi-circle perimeter, surrounded by the Claymores and trip flares. During the night we heard noises all around us, but no voices. The flares were never tripped, and we never saw any movement on the trail, in the bushes, or in the trees behind us. I made sure every man maintained extra vigilance, with rifles ready and hands on the Claymore plungers, but told them not to detonate them unless we actually heard voices or saw movement.

Luckily, we never set off any of the Claymores, and in the morning we realized just how fortunate we were. If we had set them off we would have been killed or seriously wounded. The noises we heard obviously were made by the enemy, hoping we would set off our Claymores because they had managed sneak up to them and turn them around to face us, without our knowing it. When we realized what happened, we were all visibly shaken by how close we came to being blown to bits. Following that incident, we purposely booby-trapped each of the Claymores to prevent the same thing from happening again. Any attempt to pull them out of the ground would activate a pressure switch that would trigger the Claymore. If we had no contact, we would deactivate the pressure switches before removing the mines.

On a platoon-size ambush we got into a pretty heavy firefight, and our platoon leader called for artillery support. He gave the coordinates to the artillery unit back at the base and requested one round to be fired for accuracy — a common practice. Either the lieutenant screwed up the coordinates or one of the artillery men did, because the round fell extremely short. So short, in fact, that it landed right in the middle of our position. Miraculously, it did not explode. It happened so fast, I didn't realize what was happening. I heard its whistling sound getting louder as it approached, but instead of continuing past our position, the whistling was replaced with a whoosh, flowed by a loud thud. The artillery shell had burrowed into the ground close enough to a few of us that we could reach out and touch it. If it had exploded, there's no doubt we would have been statistics. But it was a dud, defective in some way, which prevented it from detonating. Was it a miraculous incident or just plain luck?

A similar short round incident occurred on a recon mission in a pretty dense area suspected of being a Viet Cong staging area. As we got close, we heard voices and could smell food cooking, but the foliage was too thick to determine how many VC were there. Rather than take any chances, we moved a safe distance away and called in artillery. One round exploded in the tall trees directly above our position, yet not a single man was struck by the rain of shrapnel that fell. And once again, the question of luck versus something else was in my mind.

A few other friendly fire incidents that I was involved in did result in casualties, but fortunately no deaths. One such occurrence was when two of our Cobra helicopter gunships fired rockets at us. It was a two-squad recon mission and we were walking down a trail on one side of a long ridge. Unknown to us, a column of NVA soldiers was going down the other side of the same ridge, and as one of our Hueys (Bell UH-1 helicopter) flew over the ridge it took fire from the NVA. Although the door gunners could have easily returned fire, the chopper pilot immediately took evasive action and flew out of range of the incoming stream of bullets. As it turned away from the ridge, two Cobra gunships that had been hiding inside nearby clouds flew in to attack the enemy, who stopped firing and got out of sight the moment they saw the Cobras jump out of their cloud cover. We saw the gunships heading in our direction, thinking they had their sights on the other side of the ridge. But the only movement the lead gunship pilot saw was us, and before we had a chance to let him know we were friendly troops, the chopper came swooping down the trail we were on and let loose with his rockets. There was immediate chaos with everyone trying to get off the trail and behind trees. Our radio man threw out smoke grenades to mark our position and tried making contact with our rear command. But the second gunship also fired rockets before they realized we were the good guys. As the rocket barrages hit, shrapnel flew in all directions, concussions from the blasts literally blew us off our feet, and almost everyone got hit.

All of the men were wearing soft *boonie* hats, except one. He was wearing his steel helmet, which was something he rarely did. A pretty good size piece of shrapnel hit his helmet dead center above his eyebrows, but it didn't penetrate the metal. All he wound up with was a minor concussion and a bad headache; there was no

11

doubt whatsoever that the helmet saved his life. The unanswered question, of course, is what made him wear his helmet that particular day. Did he have some type of premonition that made him grab it at the last minute? He never talked about it after coming back from a short hospital stay.

I was in more firefights than I care to think about, any of which could have resulted in my getting killed, but one particular incident was like nothing I could have ever imagined happening. Even though we had a few guys who were exceptionally good point men and often volunteered for it, I felt I should not assign my men to do anything I wouldn't do myself. So on one of our platoon-size recon missions I decided it was time for me to be the point man. It was on an early December morning, my squad was leading the patrol and I was on point. We had been flown by chopper to a spot about ten klicks (a klick is one kilometer, just over six-tenths of a mile) from our base camp. We had to jump off the helicopters into some pretty thick elephant grass but we made it into the woods without incident. We walked along a trail thick with branches, vines, and underbrush, which limited visibility considerably. I was about ten or so yards ahead of the rest of my squad when the trail took a slight curve to the right. As I cautiously followed it around, I was suddenly facing a young NVA soldier who had just turned onto my trail from a smaller cross trail. We could not have been more than 20 feet from each other. My M-16 rifle was on full automatic and the safety was off, but the barrel was pointed slightly downward. If I fired, the best I could have hoped for was to hit him in the legs. His AK-47 was pointing directly at my chest, so firing without raising my rifle would have meant instant death for me. And if I raised my rifle he could shoot me before I could get him, so I just froze. The closest man behind me saw that I had stopped, but because of the curve in the trail he couldn't see why, so he stopped and motioned for the guys behind him to do the same. The NVA soldier and I stared at each other for what seemed like an eternity

12

but was actually no more than a second or two. Then he just lowered his rifle, quickly turned back to the trail he had turned off of, and just continued on that trail. I immediately ducked down into the brush and counted about a dozen NVA soldiers as they followed their point man and walked right past my trail. I stayed hidden in the bushes for a while after they passed just to be sure there weren't any others lagging behind. As soon as I was certain they were all well past me, I moved back to our platoon leader's position and reported the NVA movement, but without mentioning my encounter with the enemy point man.

After a disagreement with my commanding officer over using sound combat tactics versus what I believed was an emotional decision on his part, I was transferred to the Brigade Civil Affairs Unit as the NCO-IN-Charge. The goal of the army's Civil Affairs effort was *To Seal the Victory* in the so-called secure areas of Vietnam by *Winning the Hearts and Minds* of the Vietnamese People. This was to be accomplished by helping the civilian population in the nearby friendly villages improve the quality of their lives, mainly through Medcaps (Medical Civil Action Programs), humanitarian efforts, and recreational activities, such as movies. My duties also included assisting the PSYOP Units with their propaganda missions, which included leaflet distribution and live audio broadcasts from the air. Those propaganda techniques were used in an attempt to persuade the local population to support their nationally elected government, the Government of South Vietnam in Saigon, and to convince the VC they should surrender and change their loyalties.

My last PSYOP mission was the day my chopper got shot down, less than a month before my scheduled departure from Vietnam. The PSYOP missions were plotted based on where intelligence reports indicated suspected VC-controlled areas were located, and they were almost always heavily wooded. There were

13

always six of us on board, the pilot and copilot, two door gunner, a Vietnamese interpreter who broadcasted the messages over a thousand-watt speaker system, and me. My job was to dump the propaganda leaflets out of an open chopper door when we were over the target area. We loaded up the leaflets, tested the speaker system, and took off around mid-morning from one end of the long base runway.

On that day, the pilot did a wide 180-degree turn, and climbed to about 500 feet. As the chopper flew parallel to the runway we had taken off from, but in the opposite direction, we started receiving very heavy 51-caliber machine gun fire from the woods below. The loud noise from the engines and rotors normally muffled the sound of ground fire, but anytime our door gunners began firing their machine guns, I knew the enemy was trying to shoot us down. Within seconds after our door gunners started firing on that day, red lights flashed on the cockpit instrument panel, loud beeping noises, like the piercing sound of a smoke alarm, filled the air, and the sound of the engine changed. At least one of the rounds had knocked out our engine. The Huey was designed so the rotor blades could auto-gyrate if the engine loses power, but normally the helicopter has to be at a higher altitude than we were at for auto-gyrate to work. We should have fallen out of the sky straight down like a giant rock, but thanks to the pilot's exceptional piloting skills, we didn't. He was pulling up on the control stick that was between his knees while the co-pilot flipped switches on the front panel. We were going down pretty fast, but he somehow managed to execute another 180-degree turn and maneuver the chopper around to the opposite end of the runway that we took off from. The chopper's skids did hit the ground very hard just as we got to the edge of the runway, and then we bounced a couple of hundred of feet back into the air. This hitting hard and bouncing up continued down the entire length of the runway, with each bounce not as quite as high as the previous one. We came to a stop at

14

almost the exact spot we took off from just a few chilling minutes before.

We scrambled off as fast as we could get ourselves moving, wondering if the helicopter might explode any second from the impacts and leaking fuel. The crash crew arrived and immediately hosed down the chopper just in case. As we looked at some pretty big holes in the side of the helicopter we thought it was miraculous it hadn't crashed and burned. Many helicopters did get shot down in Vietnam, and often from much less damage than ours sustained. It was a frightening experience and it took quite a while before I calmed down.

The next morning, when my Lieutenant told me I was scheduled for another PSYOP mission later that day, I flat-out refused. Even under the threat of a Court Martial, I told him I was not leaving the base under any circumstances until my processing-out day. Nothing ever came of his threats, and my last days there were mainly spent eating sleeping, and reliving my experiences since arriving in Vietnam. And, of course, my mind was filled with questions. Why didn't the helicopter crash and burn? Why didn't we set off the Claymores the night we heard noises during the ambush? What about that dud artillery shell and the one that bombarded the area with shrapnel from above that never touched a single man? And, of course, there was that face-to-face encounter with the NVA point man? Was it simply luck or just coincidence that I walked away unscathed from those incidents. Or could life actually be predestined? Do I have a guardian angel watching over me? Do such things really exist?

Why do some men walk away untouched while others aren't as fortunate? Why didn't the NVA point man shoot me? Why did he let me live? Why does one man walk away from a firefight unscathed while the two guys practically shoulder to shoulder on

15

either side of him get wounded or killed? Why them and not the guy in the middle? Why does nothing happen to one man who picks up something off of the trail as a souvenir, while someone else does the very same thing and loses an arm or his life to a booby-trap? Why does one guy get sick minutes before going out on a mission and the helicopter he would have been on crashes, killing all those on board?

And now, more than 50 years after Vietnam, those age-old questions of, "Why am I still alive?" and "What is my purpose in life?" still haunt me. I truly believe I should have died in Vietnam, yet I didn't. Why didn't I? Who or what kept me alive, and for what purpose? I want to believe that I was saved from an early death for a reason. And if that's the case, maybe it was to help my fellow warriors and those who care about them. I'll never know for sure, but it is that possibility that has led me to write my story.

A book...*A Never-Ending Battle, How Vietnam Changed Me Forever*, describes my Vietnam experiences, the constant struggles and setbacks I went through after returning home and how I was finally rescued from the grips of Post Traumatic Stress Disorder. I believe reading my book will help families of combat veterans better understand the difficulties their loved ones go through trying to readjust to civilian life, and how they might be able to help them make that transition easier.

John Stryker Meyer

US Army Special Forces
MACV-SOG
Recon Team (RT) Idaho
1968-70
Vietnam, Southeast Asia

"Memories"

Today, in 2024, my thoughts of that country so far away from America are dramatically different from my mindset upon landing in Cam Ranh Bay in late April 1968; as I exited the airliner to be greeted by the extreme heat, humidity, rice-paddy-fecal-matter stench that permeated the air we breathed and the fear that "every Vietnamese could be a Viet Cong," as our Army trainers had cautioned us when we ran through basic and advanced infantry training.

Today, my mindset isn't on the extreme danger of running top-secret missions across the fence far behind enemy lines into Laos, Cambodia and North Vietnam where our MACV-SOG

Recon teams suffered extreme casualties at the hands of the communists. Nor on the horrific life-and-death firefights with the NVA soldiers that our recon team had.

No, today as I reflect on my 19 months of service in Southeast Asia, my mind recalls the beauty of the country, especially when flying over it in helicopters, the amazing South Vietnamese men I served with and the fearless/peerless South Vietnamese Air Force pilots and crews of the 219th Special Operations Squadron — our beloved "Kingbees" who saved our recon team time and time again against extreme odds.

First, the South Vietnamese men of our MACV-SOG Recon Team Idaho – a team wiped out twice during the eight-year secret war fought from 1964–1972: Sau, Hiep, Quang, Phouc, Son, Chau, Hung, Tuan, Cau, Vo and Minh. I had to earn their respect as we rebuilt RT Idaho, and when we ran missions, I never had to worry about my back. They were fearless. I'm alive today thanks to their courage under oftentimes heavy enemy fire power. As our team came together, I got to know them on a personal level, we mourned when Sau's wife lost their son in childbirth. We learned how Quang, Phouc and Tuan moved south from North Vietnam to get away from Ho Chi Minh's communist government. The men on RT Idaho preferred living under South Vietnam's government, knowing it was corrupt, but still preferring to die fighting for it rather than living under the thumb of corrupt communists.

Additionally, as our team grew together the camaraderie and team spirit grew, enjoying trips to Hue during a break in training or taking a lunch break in the local village café just north of FOB 1 off Highway One in Phu Bai during morning and afternoon local patrols. There were the impromptu meals in our Vietnamese team room that they'd cook up, or in the morning having a hot cup of coffee they brewed and flavored with cream and so much sugar I imagined the spoon could stand up in it. Then there were the Vietnamese poker games that could only be played by four people as each man was dealt 13 cards which the player then sorted into two five-card hands and one three-card hand in an effort to win two of the three hands played.

During the end of my first and second tours of duty at CCN in Da Nang, I most usually ate dinner with the Vietnamese men on the team in their indigenous mess as we simply enjoyed our time together, often after intense volleyball games in the sand. Both of the bases where we ran missions from were sandy, absent the red soil so prevalent throughout Vietnam, such as the historic Khe Sanh fire base the NVA hammered in early 1968. The camaraderie of those meals still provide rich memories for me, where we'd enjoy their food while exchanging verbal barbs back and forth before heading back to the team room to play some Vietnamese poker or to prepare for the next mission. Last, but not least, when RT Idaho pulled guard duty at CCN or up on top of Marble Mountain, next to our base, there would be time spent on guard but still moments getting to know more stories of team mates and while watching them mature into young men, hardened warriors. Again, upon reflection today, those were enjoyable times spent with the men of RT Idaho.

Once we got to know the South Vietnamese people, there were similarities we all shared: a love of life, food and concerns about the war of course, and sharing observations of any lovely ladies the team may have observed during the day, either on base or when we were patrolling outside the base.

And then there was the jungle and beauty of the countryside, even the land scarred by bomb craters. Flying up from Da Nang to Phu Bai or north from Phu Bai to Hue, the land had its own rich colors and landscape, rice paddies, and even the

19

cemeteries were unique with the clearly different construction of burial sites for men and women. When we flew west from S. Vietnam into Laos or Cambodia, I always admired the dark green verdant jungle, streams and hillsides which brought back memories of time I spent in the hills of my Garden State and the White Mountains of New Hampshire. Or, of the fields from my cousin's and grandfather's fields and pastures in central New Jersey. I loved the beaches of Nha Trang and Da Nang.

On one flight over the DMZ, as we headed west toward Laos, we came across a beautiful waterfall. It was so attractive the helicopter pilot turned back to circle over it a time or two as we marveled at its natural beauty and remarked that were we not engaged in a deadly war such a bucolic setting would net big bucks from tourists around the world.

Last, but certainly not least, there were the Green Berets and the American aviators and crew members that I served with during my time in country. To this day, every man I meet I judge against the men I served with in Vietnam. There were many who come to mind today in a flash: Robert J. "Spider" Parks, Pat Watkins, Doug "The Frenchman" LeTourneau, Lynne M. "Blackjack" Black, Jr., John McGovern, Rick Howard, Henry "Dick" Thompson, Don Wolken, John "Bubba" Shore, John Ingles, Eldon Bargewell, John T. Walton, John E. Peters, Garrett Robb to name a few.

Among the aviators that we actually met and worked with are: Mike "The Judge" Arline, Dan "The Executioner" Cook, William "Berg" Garlow and Jerry Herman of the "The Muskets" from the 176th Aviation Company (Assault Helicopters) from the Americal Division; Marine Corps HML-367 "Scarface"; the 101st Airmobile gunships and Cobra helicopters; the 1st Cavalry; and the amazing aviators we never met who flew the Douglas A-1

Skyraider, especially the fearless SPAD pilots from the Air Force's Operation Location Alpha Alpha detachment in Da Nang that was part of the 56th Special Operations Wing. And, of course, Kingbee Pilots Captain Nguyen Van Tuong, Captain Thinh Dinh, Lieutenants Trong and Trung, and Captain "Steve" Duong Ngoc Nhu.

The memories of those heroic, fearless men, the beauty of Southeast Asia from the air — unless anti-aircraft artillery was trying to shoot down our helicopter over Laos or Cambodia — and those beaches I shall carry with me to my grave eternally grateful for having served with them in a war against communism.

(**Author Note**): John Stryker Meyer served two tours of duty with the top-secret MACV-SOG SOF during the eight-year secret war. He has penned three non-fiction books: ***Across The Fence, The Secret War in Vietnam – Expanded Edition***; ***On The Ground, The Secret War in Vietnam***, and ***SOG Chronicles Volume One***. Meyer also hosts SOG-related podcasts entitled SOGCast: Untold Stories of MACV-SOG on YouTube, Apple and Spotify, sponsored by **Jocko Willink Productions.**

Craig Aper
Avionics Technician
Sergeant
3 Avionics Maintenance Squadron
US Air Force
Bien Hoa Air Force Base
1968 - 69

"Memories Of My War In Vietnam"

We had the *Stars and Stripes* newspaper and the Armed Forces Radio and Television but the printed articles and broadcasted programs looked nothing like what was printed by many national newspapers and reported by Walter Cronkite and others at home. Both were readily available around the base and we primarily read the paper and watched the news in the comfort of our bunk or bar in our barracks. For amusement we could cross the street to the Airman's Club for some drinks and live entertainment — usually a group from the Philippines — that could do great imitations of popular bands and songs of the day but spoke little English, if at all.

We had a primitive swimming pool and an active PX or Post Exchange for purchasing various sundries like civilian T-shirts, toothpaste and cookies, among other things. I don't remember exactly how but we could order suits made in Hong Kong, electronic equipment from Japan and even buy property in the US. We had three hot square meals a day at our chow hall and if we worked nights, we could go to the chow hall around 10 pm and get our eggs cooked anyway we liked them. Everything was made fresh at that time to be served for breakfast the next morning, although our milk was always reconstituted as, periodically, were the eggs. Until Tet in 1968 we could even leave the base and go for a drink or socialize in town. (As an aside, we usually got a heads up for a later rocket or mortar attach when the Vietnamese chow hall personnel didn't show up for work.)

Occasionally, we were able to arrange for fresh stakes and eggs from the Saigon neighborhood of Cholon markets — both legitimate and black. Usually, we had hot running water for showers, shaving and teeth brushing but, sometimes potable water was hard to come by. I remember brushing my teeth with beer or soda from time to time.

This is all to say, we in the Air Force fought a much different kind of war than our compatriots in the Army and Marines in the field. This was brought home to me when somehow my good friend Chad Spawr was able to find me amongst all the chaos. He was particularly delighted that he could take a hot shower after days, maybe, weeks without one in the field. He was entertained at our service club and seemed to regain some of his humanity and his spirit perked up during his all too brief visit.

We did have a war, complete with Donut Dollies — just different. We were frequently shelled in Bien Hoa and were extremely busy engaged in our primary mission of close air support for I Corp and 3 Corp. We had 3, F-100 jets constantly on alert status prepared to be airborne within five minutes. I am proud to report we were always able to ensure an alert aircraft did not have to abort a mission because of radio equipment failure. It took as much as fifteen minutes or more to bring up a fighter from the reserves — time that was critical for the troops on the ground engaged in life threatening fire fights. We also maintained communications equipment for "Puff the Magic Dragon," the C-47 gunships, F-37 spotter planes, C-130 herbicide birds and transport planes and the occasional visitor from another airbase.

We were shelled fairly frequently, mostly at night, although the "incoming" tended to be light. I always believed that the primary reason we were shelled was to cause us to be awaked, to run to the bunkers and keep us sleep deprived so we would make more mistakes that would have disastrous consequences for troops in the field. Still, I will never forget the sounds of the alert siren rudely awakening us. More frightening, however, was to be awakened by ordinance whistling overhead or exploding nearby. Always there was a moment of panic as we jumped into our boots, grabbed our helmets and flack vest and ran to the bunker, someone invariably yelling hit the bunker, hit the bunker — as if we needed a reminder of what to do.

Every now and then I would be out working on the flight line when we would be attacked. If I was already in a hardened bunker for an aircraft I could remain in place, if not I had memorized the locations of many bunkers near where I would be working. On one occasion a buddy and I stopped to chat with a flight-line security guard, as we often did to help them stay awake and alert, when we all saw a flash of light from across the runways. The security guard said something then grabbed the two of us and rolled behind the sandbags that made up the four low walls of his post, along with a tin roof. Lucky for us he recognized what was happening and the danger as our bomb storage area exploded, slamming the bags into us as shrapnel rained down all around.

On another occasion, I was driving the repair truck around an unfamiliar part of the base when the shelling started. I quickly stopped the truck and spotted a convenient sandbag shelter. Only later, while driving in the same area during daylight did I see the danger sign stipulating this was a napalm storage area — sometimes you just get lucky.

Mostly I was always a little queasy when I had to work on a C-130 at night. They were parked in a low light area, did not have bunkers around them, and were very close to the perimeter of the base and close to where many of the rockets and mortars were launched. I distinctly remember being on a rolling ladder approximately 30 feet in air fixing the antenna wiring in the tip of the tail while a light was shining up at me and I could see the perimeter guards with their dogs. I gave some serous though about sliding down the handrails if we were shelled.

Besides the sirens, the flight-line tower would broadcast an alert anytime we were under attack. One night I was following one

25

of my buddies into a C-130 when immediately upon plugging in his headset he turned, jumped over my head, and stared running for a bunker while shouting incoming so I would follow — he'd heard the broadcast from the tower in his headset. We were in an unfamiliar area and were shouting back and forth trying to locate a bunker. Shortly after entering a bunker, an agitated security guard came in and told us it was only because we were shouting in English about trying to find a bunker that he did not fire at us. I never did know whether he was serious or just jacking us up. As I said, sometimes you get lucky.

Somethings will remain for me forever: the sounds B-52's dropping tons of 500-pound bombs near-by, something I think they called carpet bombing; the deep "brrrrrat" sounds of gunships as they fired on nearby Vietcong or North Vietnamese Regulars; the sounds of the sirens or rockets or mortars exploding. For me, the fright of those occasions has fortunately diminished over time such that I don't jump and look for a bunker when I hear sirens or loud noises. Sometimes, however, when I least expect it, the memories do flood over me.

To my fellow service members, especially those that fought in the fields, I want to say thank you, God Bless you, and welcome home.

Tony Kay
Vietnam Veteran
US Army Security Agency

Author's Note: *I wrote the following letter to the Detroit Free Press in February of 1987. They asked Vietnam veterans to write in after they had seen the movie "Platoon" which had just been released. Keep in mind...home computers were not a commodity at that time.*

I am writing this letter with word processing software on a small computer that I own. I suppose you could consider me successful with a stable life like the vast majority of my fellow Vietnam Veterans. Unfortunately, however, there is also a sizable minority who have been severely scarred both physically and/or mentally by the war.

I served in country from June of 1968 to June of 1969, and to some I had it easy. I was with an Army Intelligence unit that, because of the sensitive nature of the material and equipment, required that I work in a windowless cinder block air-conditioned building.

I can hear all the guffaws now from the grunts, but wait guys, give me a break. Part of my job was to read the daily action reports that came in during the night and condense them into a briefing for the officers who came in early in the morning. Then I went back to my billet to "sleep in the heat" and mark another day off the calendar.

For the better part of a year, I got to read about each incident in II Corps (central Vietnam). From major operations to historically insignificant but just as deadly small skirmishes, the war passed in written form before my eyes. I know what it was like out in the field from these reports and from talking to the guys who were out there.

I got so depressed by the never-ending litany of KIA, WIA numbers that I learned how to shut everything out and for a while, even stopped writing home, much to the dismay of my folks.

The irony of my experiences is that while the area I was in could be considered safe and normal, the safety was relative to that in the jungle. Compared to the world back home, you would not consider it safe or normal to see dead bodies in the street, the victims of terrorist snipers, satchel charge bombs, or even inadvertently dropped "friendly" grenades or stray rifle rounds (in reality, grenades and bullets have no friends).

There was no way while I was in Nam that I was going to volunteer to go out in the field. Yet, I spent the entire year continuously "wired" because of the potential for violence all around me.

The year was so intense and it was such a relief to see it end that a guy sitting next to me on the plane home said, "I don't care if this plane crashes in the middle of the Pacific Ocean, at least I didn't get killed in Nam." That statement did and still does make absolutely perfect sense to me.

I came home with a classic case of survivor's guilt. On the one hand the people here, though well meaning, couldn't relate to the environment of insanity, chaos, waste, stress, and depression that I had been subjected to for a year. At the same time, I didn't really feel that my "war experiences" were adequately terrible enough to talk about with a fellow vet for fear that he might laugh at how easy I had it. (Not much chance of that happening in 1969 however, because none of us were talking back then.)

About 1983, I met a vet who in 1969 was paralyzed from the waist down by a sniper's bullet. It was only through talking with him that I was able to get it together with respect to my emotions about the war.

One day he said to me, "Tony, there were only two safe places in Vietnam." I thought, "Uh oh, here it comes, I am really going to get slam dunked now because he is going to say Cam Ranh Bay and Tan Son Nhut and I was stationed at the latter." I said, "Where was that, Lee?" He said, "Underneath the soles of both your feet."

He truly convinced me that he wasn't a hero because he was an ex-infantry man in a wheelchair and I deserved his respect even though I had a rear echelon job. He just happened to be unlucky enough to get wounded while I was lucky enough to survive able bodied. I mean here is this guy in a wheelchair telling me not to sweat it because every place over there was dangerous. It put things into perspective.

When I was there, I shared with grunts the confusion, fear, loneliness and anguish that they felt. And I most certainly will

29

never forget the looks on the faces of the new arrivals that were getting off the plane that was to take me home.

Wars are an unfortunate reality in this world. Many people pay lip service to the sacrifices that must be periodically made to preserve our freedom and I fear that they are ready to charge off onto some crusade not fully aware of the consequences.

I have seen the movie "Platoon." I hope the movie will remind today's youth and today's flag wavers that those sacrifices are stark and real. They should not be incurred lightly. You had better be damned sure that the cause you are fighting for is really worth the price that will inevitably be paid.

My paralyzed friend died in 1984 of complications arising from his war injury. Twenty years later and we are still burying the dead. While not a recurring nightmare, I play the tape of this action in my head often.

Jeffrey Holst
LT(jg) Jeffrey R. Holst – In Country 9/69 to 9/70
River Division 531 & Advisor to River Patrol Group 57
(Vietnam Navy)

Saigon River – Several Klicks Upriver From Phu Cuong – October 1969

Our two river patrol boats (PBR) from Navy River Division 531 have set up a "waterborne guard post" (better known as an ambush) on the bank of the river where we suspect Charles has been crossing. It is pitch black, no moon, and with the exception of constant chatter from all kinds of bugs, it is really quiet. We're tucked under some overhanging trees…waiting.

I hear a movement and pick up the starlight scope; don't see anything. Ah, it's probably a monkey or some other animal. Then I hear it again, and this time I know Charles is there. I pick up the starlight scope again, and there they are, several of the little fuckers about 10 feet from our boat. I don't know if they didn't see us or were trying to get close enough to throw a satchel into our boat.

I whispered to the Boat Captain, "Time to get the hell out of here." He nodded, touched the forward gunner (twin .50 cal machine guns) on the shoulder, and put the gates on the pumps that drove the boat into reverse before starting the engines. I touched the waist gunner's shoulder (M-60) and pointed in the direction of the gooks. The Boat Captain started the engines (2 6V53 GMC diesels driving two large pumps), and we opened fire as the boat leaped back into the river.

While our boat was firing, and Charles was shooting at us, there was nothing happening with our sister boat. I kept calling on the radio, "Shapeless 11 Alpha, this is 11, pull back and open up." The last thing I wanted to happen was a friendly fire situation. It turns out that boat would not start. The whole thing was over in a matter of seconds, although it felt much longer. They missed...we didn't.

As you might imagine, the boat engineer for 11A got a serious ass chewing. Little did I know that when we turned our boats over to the VN navy and I became a senior advisor, this would be a regular occurrence.

When the tunnels at Cu Chi were discovered, it confirmed that we were spot on about selecting this location to interdict Charles; the tunnel complex was just a klick inland from the bank opposite from our ambush-site.

(Author Note):
Jeff and I worked together at Kennametal in Pennsylvania. We were professional colleagues and friends. He passed away in February 2021. Miss him every day!

Marty Hauser
Firebase C2, Near the DMZ
1970 – 71

"Night Guard Duty In A Combat Environment"

It was only my second day with B - Battery and I was assigned to guard duty. It was me, my buddy Dan, and one of the other guys that had already been in country for a while. I was nervous, scared, and didn't know what to do or what to expect.

We were taken out to the OP. It was a two story tower and a 50 caliber machine gun on the top floor and an M-60 machine gun on the bottom floor. The top floor of the tower was completely open and the bottom floor only had little slits to fire out of and to see out of. The bottom portion of the tower was also used for sleeping and was one cot in there.

It was around 4:00 pm when we got to the OP and the older guy (I call him "the older guy" only because he had been "In

Country" longer than I, not because he was actually older than I), explained what was expected of us. He gave us a five minute lesson on how to fire a 50 caliber and an M-60, neither of which I had ever touched before, so I was a little lost. He told us he would take first watch and that we should decide which of us would take second watch and let him know so that he knew who to wake. Then he instructed us that if a trip flare went off we should just open fire on it.

I had third watch and tried to sleep but couldn't. I was just too nervous not knowing what was going to happen. Then my turn came to watch. The password was given to me and I went to the top of the tower. I had never seen more blackness in my life. Black enough that you couldn't even see the perimeter wire. My eyes felt like they got larger from straining to see through the darkness and I thought I was seeing images that weren't actually there.

Then the noises started and I could almost feel my ears growing larger from straining to hear. I was sitting there all tensed up and my body was tight and my hands were on the 50 caliber ready to fire. There was nothing happening, but in my young mind, I was sure that the shit was going to start any minute! Then I began to wonder if I was going to handle it and it I would do the right things in any given situation.

As my watch went on and I was sitting there, I suddenly heard a noise behind me. I almost came "unglued!" Then I remembered my guard duty training. I made the person identify himself and give me the password. Believe it or not, I actually did it right and felt a little better.

My watch that night seemed like an eternity. I finally started to see the sunrise on another day and told myself that I made it through that first night (with a sigh of relief). As the days went by and I pulled more guard duty, I became more accustomed to all the sounds and learned with were good sounds and which were bad sounds. The nights still remained so black that I couldn't see five feet in front of me, but I learned to relax (if that's what you want to call it) enough to at least take my hands off the 50-Cal!

Jim Gaertner
Point-man
C/1/12 1st Cavalry Division
1969 - 1972

"It Don't Mean Nothin'…"

We used to say that a lot in Vietnam. At the end of the day after humping an 85-90 pound rucksack plus weapons and ammo, and every muscle and bone in your body aches? "It don't mean nothin'……"

Wearing the same ragged, filthy, sweat-soaked jungle fatigues for weeks and weeks on end without being able to bathe like a normal human being? "It don't mean nothin'……"

Living in the jungle like an animal, becoming one with them by necessity to survive? "It don't mean nothin'……"

Walking point down a well-travelled enemy trail, smelling the cooking fires of the enemy, sensing their presence but unable to

36

see much because of the thick jungle foliage? "It don't mean nothin'……"

Pulling your watch (guard duty) at the gun position (M-60 machine gun) in the middle of the night in darkness so black you can't see your hand in front of your face, listening to the night sounds of the jungle and wondering if "Charlie" is out there stealthily crawling up on your position to kill you, you silently praying for daylight? "It don't mean nothin'……"

Getting a "Dear John" letter from your wife or steady girlfriend back home? "It don't mean nothin'……"

Firefights and cries of "Medic!" "God!" "Jesus!" "Mommy!"...cries that will haunt you all the days of your life? "It don't mean nothin'……"

Watching good men die, including a best buddy, powerless to do anything for them, telling them they're gonna be O.K. when you know they're not? "It don't mean nothin'……"

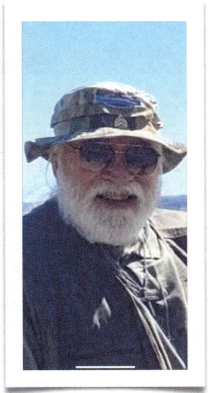

It don't mean nothin'……?

WHY did we say that? We said it because we hurt so bad no other words would come. We said it because we couldn't afford the luxury to grieve, to cry. "It don't mean nothin'," you say……?

No, it meant everything EVERYTHING! That is all.

Chad Spawr
US Army, Vietnam October 1967 to July 1969
1st Infantry Division
MACV Advisory Team 47
6th PSYOP Battalion
2d Brigade 1st Cavalry Division (Airmobile)

"Incoming"

The Quan Loi basecamp was a fairly large combat base built around a 3500-foot dirt runway in the middle of a French rubber plantation. Located about sixty miles north of Saigon, a few miles east of Highway 13 (Thunder Road) and about fifteen miles south of the Cambodian border, Quan Loi was an operating base in 1968 for the 1st Brigade of the 1st Infantry Division. At least five battalions of infantry, armor, several artillery, aviation, and related support units were based at Quan Loi.

Our barracks consisted of GP Medium tents draped over 2x4 timber frames; each could accommodate about a dozen soldiers. The tents, or "hooches," were aligned between the rows of rubber trees; on hot days, the rubber provided cooling shade; during mortar and rocket attacks, the rubber provided a rain of shrapnel from enemy fire exploding in the foliage.

On the evening of January 31, 1968, the Communists launched their Tet Offensive. In addition to attacking almost every town and city in Vietnam, they also fired large concentrations into American basecamps in an attempt to tie our troops down to prevent us from going on the offensive to defeat their attacks. These attacks, for the most part, only delayed the dispatch of combat troops to the places needed to recapture territory from the enemy. Within a few days, major American and Allied forces were dispatched to those places to fight back the VC and NVA troops.

The first night at Quan Loi was remarkable for the number and types of ordnance thrown at the basecamp. In addition to hundreds of 82-mm mortar rounds, we were hit with large numbers of 107-mm and 122-mm rockets. To the extent these could be aimed by the enemy, they were "focused" on troop housing areas, with hundreds of rounds also fired at our flight-line to disable or destroy our fleet of Huey helicopters. At least one enemy rocket hit a basecamp ammo dump, setting off a huge explosion. Fortunately, it was mostly small arms ammo, and we had plenty of that on hand.

The next morning, we began assessing the damage inflicted, and I was surprised that it wasn't much worse. While we were hearing of a few casualties caused by mortar rounds, the actual physical damage was minimal. A few empty tents were struck, but as they were unoccupied, there was little real damage. I remember picking up pieces of rocket shrapnel, metal strips about twelve inches in length, but with razor sharp edges. Those could cut down a tree or sever an arm of leg. In several other places, I found the tails of exploded mortar rounds imbedded in the dirt. This seemed curious at the time, but when a mortar round explodes, its downward energy and trajectory will overcome the blast effect of the exploding round and the tail will then bury itself in the ground. I collected about a half dozen of these tails. All had Chinese or Russian markings on the tail fins. They were strange souvenirs.

I traded a few here or there for other souvenirs, keeping one last tail for myself. As it turned out, when I was wounded in 1969 and sent through the hospital system to recover, some enterprising soldier in my unit apparently found my mortar tail and liberated it, along with most of my other war souvenirs.

During the first several days of Tet '68, Quan Loi took hundreds of rockets and mortars in a continuous barrage. At one point, our Brigade Sergeant Major commented that over a thousand incoming rounds had been counted in the last twenty-four hours.

After a few days, we received a "counter-battery" radar that could be used to track incoming enemy fire and coordinate instantly with our artillery and heavy mortar batteries to return fire. In addition, several Huey gunships would take off straight up and hover over the basecamp without their lights. As soon as they saw the flash of a mortar tube, they could open fire before the enemy could break down the tube and run. There were occasional secondary explosions in the bush, indicating that our return fire had been effective, but for a few weeks the incoming enemy fire only slackened slightly.

There were several times later in my tours when I came under mortar and rocket attack, but I guess the Fates weren't interested in collecting my hide. Although I grew accustomed to the sound of mortar tubes firing and hearing the rounds flying inbound, it was harder to become so "unaffected" by Chinese rockets. These were usually launched from several miles away, so we couldn't hear the actual launches. The general rule was that if you could hear the round coming, you weren't in real danger. It was the ones you didn't hear that had your name on them. They were literally terrifying.

One of my recurring nightmares (now more than fifty-five years later) is the sound of a mortar tube firing. Something will happen in a dream and I'll "hear" that sound, and I panic myself awake. It takes a few minutes to calm down, realizing that it was a dream, but it is still there. There are noises that happen that sometimes sound like a tube firing, and they always get my attention.

William "Doc" Forgey
Former S4 4th PSYOP Group (and 6th Battalion before transition into the 4th Group)
RVN Aug. 1966 — Dec. 1968

...As you may know, I spent 30 consecutive months in Vietnam Working as either the S-4 or assistant S-4 of the fourth psychological operations group. A lot of stuff happened during that time and in my travels constantly to our organizations in all four tactical combat zones. Here is a gentle story;

There was a logistics office in Saigon that manages the ocean transportation providing various landing times for cargo of all sorts including soldier-carrying freighters. Much of what we ordered was through special funding provided directly from the deputy chief of staff operations in Pentagon DSCOPS-International Affairs Directorate, under which UW, SOPS, PSYOPS was administratively located. This gave us unusual ability to bypass purchasing officers and virtually all segments of the transportation system. It took several years for this to establish itself and I had to explain this relationship personally as a 1st Lieutenant and then eventually as a Captain to a number of general grade officers gently as this system was being jammed down their throats by DCSOPS.

Well, one day I needed to expedite a freighter loaded with paper into the harbor at Saigon. I went to the officer in charge of the Harbor designating the ship and my request. You could tell he was pissed. Hundreds of ships were waiting and mine had just arrived. As usual it was hot and humid as hell and some of these shops were even troop transports. As he put the order causing my ship to be brought forward into the dock system for immediate unloading, he stared at me and in a very disgusted voice said: "The only two items that have priority over PSYOP paper are blood and embalming fluid." I, of course, used a very blank face as I sat there in the dealing silence that fell upon all on that office at that moment.

This event happened in the late summer or early fall 1968.

Yep, Tet in Saigon was interesting, but many other situations matched the intensity or were personally impactful when they occurred. But they are more human-interest stories like the one above and my actual scary stuff was short in duration and since the events turned out benign are meaningless to anyone else but me at that moment.

Trevor Shelley
Royal Australian Engineers
Vietnam Service...April 1966/April 1967
Unit-1 Field Troop-1 Field Squadron,
Based at Nui Dat, Phuoc Tuy Province...Ran Sapper,
Role: Field Combat Engineer embedded with Infantry
Companies - responsible for clearing tunnels and villages
Nine years in the Australian Army, also mobilized to
Papua, New Guinea, Northern Thailand and Malaysia,
Seconded to the British Army for two years as well.

"The Full Circle!"

Some years ago now, Lyndal and I went to a "mini" family reunion of the Shelley Clan! And as you do, I dived into the function boots and all. Little Bay in Sydney was the venue and there were a lot of them there! Well, Dad had a brother and a heap of sisters as well, but his bother Jack had been a POW of the Japanese. Jack and Dad were very close.

Actually, Jack was one of the first Aussies captured in Malaya up at Kota Baru with the Indian battalions who engaged the Japanese invaders first. Ironically, Dad would have been sailing past on his way home from serving in the Middle East with the 6th Division, 2nd AIF when Uncle Jack was having his first bowl of watery rice. Dad had that return trip interrupted and had to stay in Ceylon/Sri Lanka for about six weeks while everybody argued where to send them. And believe it or not, "Weary Dunlop" was on Ceylon with them.

Dad was baffled for years how the hell Weary got captured in Java. Well, as we all know now, the convoy was split after it left Ceylon and half sent to Java in an attempt to relieve the Dutch battling there but it was too late and they were all captured just about on arrival. Meanwhile, Dad sailed on into the night bound for Perth, later the Kokoda Trail and a big hole in the head during the Battle of Erowa creek. But I digress!

Uncle Jack survived the war and bloody well survived the Thai Burma Railway. He was released from the Camps around Nagasaki in very late 1945. Life goes on and Uncle Jack married Aunty Nell and in time had three more "little Shelley's"…two girls and a boy; Jeanette, Rosemary and John…my cousins. Rosemary in particular and I tended to imbibe in some very delightful top-shelf red during the event where conversation flowed, memories hashed-over and we laughed about lots of promises about catching up again…La La La La! Rosie made the comment that someday in the future we should meet in Saigon and I chaperone Jeanette (long suffering Rosie Sister) and herself on a tour down through what is now Baria Province, but you and I know it's really Phuc Tuy…in Vietnam of course!

Rosemary and Jeanette were looking for a personal tour guide around the Australian sites and I was to be that person. Well,

Lo and Behold…March 2017 it came to fruition and we hooked up in what is to me still Saigon. HCMC is ok but! And there was more. We managed to chase up a few more starters. No young fillies or stallions mind but when I lined them all up I knew this was going to be a great trip. And Mr. Hà, the long term partner in crime, with Jim Marrett in the Tunnel Rats Tours who was thrown in for good measure who proved to be a wonderful organizer and pretty damn good to have a beer with as well. In addition to Mr Ha, Rosemary, Jeanette, Lyndal and myself, we also had Bob Alexander…very important to have Bob along as he had the bar several doors down from my house in Phnom Penh. Patricia Ayoub …very long time and dear Friend who knows Sappers so well. Married to Arab Ayoub who some referred to as Dennis, very much in a previous lifetime but to us it was always Arab. Alan "Sparra" Christie A Sapper / Tunnel Rat and a bit of an Icon around the Corp or so he will have you believe.

Of the Original 3 Fd Tp in Ben Hoa (of Cu Chi tunnels fame), I had the pleasure of going on some hikes in the big jungle with them to learn the ropes when I first arrived in Vietnam. And last but not least was Sparra's brother, Bruce, having his first tour. We will take him again after this sterling effort from him during the whole exercise. Lyndal and I had been on quite a few trips up through the Australian area in Phuoc Tuy over the years, of course me having done one more than her. On previous trips nobody went near Duc. My village and I never really bothered to ask as well. We just tagged along through the well-known spots but this time, I had Sparra with me and he had been on Operation Sydney with a different splinter team to me but he was there and If I remember rightly it was with Bruce Mckenzie.

So, "Take us to Duc My Village," was the directive and it took the driver a bit by surprise as the action there with 5 RAR early days and a pretty unusual scenario, but not well-known, and it was a pretty round about trip that got me to Duc My in the first place back in 1966. Even now I remember the interest I had in Vietnam back in the late fifties as a young fella and how I read about what the Viet Minh and French were up to while living in that small South Western NSW Hamlet (Monteagle) some 10 miles out of Young towards Cowra.

There was very little going on around Young in the way of opportunities for a growing lad so in 1964, so I threw my hands in the air and joined the Army. Little did I know that in a couple of years, I was going to come face to face with the Viet Minh, but now known as Viet Cong with the added attraction of being a couple of meters underground with a torch and pistol to soothe my nerves.

When I first enlisted, I thought that the Signal Corp would suit me, so that's what I put down on the piece of paper. But no, the Army knew better. So after recruit training, I found myself marching into SME. Lo and Behold I had become a Sapper! My route to 1 Tp, 1 Fd Sqn was by a circuitous route beginning in that Champagne posting to 17 Fd Sqn at Randwick, with all the attractions of Sydney at my fingertips. Ignoring of course all of the winter exercises at Rylstone and other such gems for the camper that put a bit of a damper on the froth. Borneo postings were available at that time, but I was too young…just a boy soldier. So instead, I was included in the Composite Troop that was posted to PNG in 1965. (Before Independence so no need for a passport to go there.)

I thought I had won the lottery, being billeted in tents near the gates of Murray Barracks in a troop of mainly experienced Sappers and some very good blokes. Port Moresby was a great town in those days and I could often be found learning my skills in the bottom pub in town…my favorite. Our main task was constructing Lysart Buildings all over the place and I suffered my first wounding in the Army there when jumping off a building I landed on a piece of timber with a 6-inch nail poking straight up and it went right through my foot.

This was followed by three very pleasant days in Port Moresby General Hospital under observation This was a great Hospital in those days. January 1966, I marched back into the 17th Construction in Randwick to find a very different scenario. They were mobilizing and training for South Vietnam with National Service just starting up. And even though I had my leg in plaster for six weeks due to a Boyle's fracture picked up at Rylston shacking with Taff Francis and others who will remain faceless, I was processed along with the rest. The plaster came off and to this day, I have had no more troubles with it.

Time flew and before I knew it, I was boarding a Qantas 707 at Richmond on Anzac Day 1966 for a flight to Manilla which connected with Air France into Saigon. We got off in Saigon but all of our kit went on to Paris and came back three weeks later. All very heady stuff for a young fella from the bush. We were picked up from Saigon in some broken down old US Aircraft and Vung Tau eventually came into view after flying through a very heavy shower, much of which came through the skin of the aircraft we were in.

"Dumped in the sand hills of Vung Tau," I soon became involved in the water point and that was a good number but boredom began to settle in, even though I was a regular at the China Doll bar. I must say though that the staff there did a lot for the morale of a fresh young country boy. Part of the diversion was watching the HMAS Sydney come into Vung Tau and all of the troops landing "packed for bear" while we sat outside the bars and watched the show.

About two weeks before Operation Sydney with 5 RAR, the Tp Sgt. of 10 Tp, 17th Construction read out a request for anybody who would like to move north to the "Dat" and join the ranks of 1 Fd Sqn. I raised my hand and very soon I was getting to know everybody in the 1 Tp lines at Nui Dat.

Mid-June it was and I remained there for the rest of my tour. At that time, 3 Fd Tp was spending its last weeks in the country and 2 Tp had not really arrived. So all of the members of 1 Tp were training as No 2's in the splinter teams with the 3 Tp Guys. We were, and did so for some time support 5RAR, 6 RAR, APC's and did lots of civil and construction works around the Dat. This included messes for the 175 guns that moved in after the Long Tan battle. Pretty full on and of course having just moved into leaky four-man tents.

The big event in the early days was the erecting of a Marque as a mess tent but things did slowly improve…even an open-air movie paddock. First feature was Nino Culotta in "Their a Weird Mob." I suppose at that time, I was very green and just after arriving in Nui Dat S/Sgt. Blair Parsons teamed me up with Doug Sanderson, whom if I remember correctly was a L/Cpl. and just completing his tour with the original 3 Fd Tp. Not so green in the ways of the Army as I had been in 18 months and had PNG under my belt, but as a Super Grunt carrying more kit than them and never even had practiced in a tunnel…well, that was a bit out there.

But Duc My is not far from Nui Dat especially now that there is a very good road going right beside it. Now all of this was fifty plus years ago and my memory isn't what is was but for those who know the area it is past Nui Dat on the way to Binh Bah, a very small hamlet in its day and mainly populated by displaced Montagnard people. Although during Operation Sydney, Nui Dat could have been a million miles away.

This being in the early days of the Vietnam War, Sappers were very seldom briefed or able to attend the "0" groups, we just turned up and did the biding of the resident Platoon Sgt. of the day. So the beginning of the operation found us moving across the foothills of Wolverton Mountains. I am pretty certain that we were delivered out there by APC. I was still a bit overawed by it all. Then we swung out into the paddy fields with some pretty heavy forested area in the distance. And I was sticking with Doug like there was no tomorrow.

About 1500 hours, the Company/platoon we were with halted and we all went to ground along the edge of the rice paddy and very close to the edge of what looked like some pretty serious jungle. Of course, we took the opportunity to rest and have a smoke. But not long after going to ground a very young 2nd Lieutenant moved amongst us instructing us all to make the most of this, rest, try and get some sleep as we would be moving out at 2100. FOR WHAT? I really had no idea. I thought I would be all snuggled up in my Hutchie by then. And it was starting to spit rain. Of course peer pressure caused me just to go along and all would become clear. "Jesus," I had just turned 19 and did not want to appear green. Doug I think had worked it out and the rain was starting to get a bit heavier.

So there we sat, waiting until 2100. Around 2030 everybody started to get organized. Moving to the edge of the forest and scratching around on forest floor like old chooks! At first I had no idea but it soon dawned on me. They were picking up pieces of bark and shoving them into their webbing at the back of the shoulder. Utilizing the properties of Florescence in decaying tree bark. To say I was unprepared for this was a bit of an understatement. I had never been to Canungra, managed to miss out after coming back from PNG and damaging my ankle. Add to that the fact that I had just turned 19 eight days before, I left so there with some argument if I should go at all. Round shoulders and skinny to boot…lucky if I was 9 stone and 7 lbs. But here I was about to embark on one of the longest nights in my life, although since then, there have been a few others as well. And the rain was steady now. And the grunts realized that the phosphorescence while worked was not ideal. So the word came back…toggle ropes and it appears everyone had one. Well, there was not a word as the order of the day was absolute silence but we all got the message. And it worked. Some adjustment at first but as we settled down in the pitch dark as it can only get in close forest without a moon with steady rain the long snake of men…a full companies worth plus a couple of Sappers gradually picked up speed to about the pace of a snail but it was steady progress. This continued for some hours and of course the ground was very broken. I had the security of being tethered to Doug, the old hand, but that's about as far as it went and I suppose like the rest of the column, we had no idea where we were and how we were going. Of course, somebody must have or we were all in trouble.

I am guessing now, but it must have been about 2 am and the rain was easing when our toggle ropes went tight and some of us were pulled to the ground. High tension lying there waiting for incoming ordinance but nothing happened. Then a very shadowy figure made his way along briefing everybody very quietly. Same 2nd Lt. that told us to take advantage of the break earlier that afternoon. And you wouldn't read about it. One of the diggers in the line a few up from us zigged instead of zagging and fell straight down a well, missing the timber cross-member and splashing into the water some 50 feet below. Other than his pride, nothing else was hurt. Twenty minutes of scratching around and he was back on the surface and ready to go. It took a little time to settle down with toggle ropes getting slack then tight but we did and continued for another couple of hours.

51

The rain had stopped now and even though we could not smell ourselves we stank from living in the bush. It's a wonder the Vietnamese in Duc My couldn't smell us coming. At last the thick country was thinning out and just the very slightest signs of dawn approaching were visible and you could hear the roosters in the village crowing and the odd dog bark. I still have vivid memories of looking down onto this small pretty basic hamlet with a very fast flowing and clear stream bisecting it. As it grew lighter, we moved into the cordon position with the companies linked up and waited. This part of the exercise had worked well. And we waited. I looked at Doug and Doug looked at me. We both looked at all the grunts and gained nothing and so we waited.

Like a house fly buzzing around your dinner while you are in the next room, I heard a buzz coming towards us but could see nothing. But wait, there it was in the distance heading directly toward us and the Buzz getting a lot louder. Suddenly it was overhead and began to circle. And at the same time its buzz was drowned out by loudspeakers attached to the aircraft. As it circled, it was instructing everyone to stay indoors and they would be OK…wishful thinking on their part! Simultaneously, the platoon Sergeant motioned us to move in and then everything went pear shaped.

The hut doors flew open and several surprised, but well-armed VC, burst forth firing as they came. It was pretty easy now…just go along with Doug and the rest, but I found myself running across an open clearing with Doug just ahead of me going into tree cover near some houses when glancing over my shoulder I noticed spurts of dirt coming towards me. I knew what it was as I had seen it a few times in Roy Rogers movies and then a quick sprint and I caught up with Doug. As the cordon was being drawn, quite a few small side actions were taking place all across the village. One of the 5 RAR guys jumped into a trench and also a well-armed VC jumped into the same trench and the same time. The good guy won and the VC was killed.

Now the following event was reported in the 5 RAR notes but very much underwhelming for the Sappers. It was played down a lot and they took most of the kudos. After quite a bit of gunfire all became quiet. Doug and I began searching houses for everything but mainly tunnel or bunker entrances. All of the residents that were not trying to kill us had been rounded up and were sitting together nearby.

We entered quite a prominent house just up from the stream and the old lady who obviously owned the house was a bit hysterical…all new stuff to me. There was an overwhelming smell of charcoal and fish paste. It was very sparsely furnished, all a bit vague now but the fireplace was prominent so of course we started poking around there. The old lady was in there with us and desperately trying to distract us away from the fireplace. I did wonder what the hell she was doing in there but of course… Eureka, pay dirt. A trapdoor under the hearth, well actually to the side of it. We were kitted up with 9-mm pistols, bayonet and a miner's type lamp with the battery clipped on our belts with a long lead with a bright light at the end of it. Doug had opened the entry and looked at me indicating we go down. There were many other occasions later of the same scenario and I became quite blasé in entering tunnels. But on this morning, I was but a virgin.

Anyhow how hard could it be? I was fortunate in a way as the tunnel was fairly high and we could walk bent over. Red Mud, as usual, and a domed roof but this was more a bunker entrance and it was not very long. Much more accessible than many others that I searched later where you were on your hands and knees or stomach a lot of the time. I kept a respectful distance behind Doug holding my pistol at the ready for whatever might eventuate. Then

53

he stopped! What was going on? He waved me forward, or I thought he had, as it was pretty dark as he was shading his torch somewhat. Yes, yes that was a hand motion I'm sure. So gingerly, I came up behind him, and Oh No…there was another branch off the main tunnel and it sure looked like he was motioning me to go and have a look.

Oh well, no longer the Virgin! So into the entrance I went. This one was a bit smaller and after traveling about 20 yards or so I came to the end of it…to my relief. Back to Doug I went, even prodded the walls a couple of times. I had heard you did that. Actually, many months later the wall prodding action paid big dividends for me in another tunnel complex a long way from this one. I motioned to Doug that it was nothing. He turned and continued on up the tunnel. It was not to long when he stopped again. Jesus, I was getting sick of this stopping caper. And yes, there was that hand again motioning me forward. Up I went and Doug was crouching this time indicating into a larger room. We had reached the bunker proper. There were timber supports as well as rafters. Doug was motioning across the tunnel and lo and behold, up in the rafters was a small Vietnamese guy trying to hide. He was bleeding profusely from the leg area. All this was happening very quickly. Doug dispatched me to the surface to fetch a tear gas canister. I made short work of that and was back in no time handing it to Doug. He never missed a beat. He pulled the pin and lobbed it across the bunker and underneath where the Viet Cong was hiding in the rafters. Doug and I then beat a hasty retreat to the surface. Once in the fresh air, we grabbed gas masks and went and sat on top of the bunker roof and waited. Below us were groans and moans, a bit of yelling and the odd scream as the tear gas in a very confined space did its work. And we waited for what seemed to be a long time but it wasn't until all noise below us had stopped that we moved.

Down we went again but this time masked up. We also had a big rifleman with us from memory to help drag him out. Doug and I were only little guys, designed for tunnels but not brute strength. It was very smokey in the tunnel and the bunker from the tear gas but eventually we could see a form on the bunker floor. It was our man and he was unconscious from the tear gas. We carefully checked him out for booby traps and the like, but this fellow was not a very sophisticated guy and only had the basic kit. We relieved him of it before the infantry, waiting outside, got to him. That's what Tunnel Rats did.

I was rewarded with a terrific hammock which I used for years, a cigarette lighter and a pretty mean looking knife with a 50 caliber round as the handle. The infantry claimed him right at the entrance and he received VIP treatment from then on, soon regained consciousness and was given water, food and cigarettes. My last memory was of this young guy sitting and leaning against a tree with a cigarette in his mouth, one leg heavily bandaged and looking very happy with the world. But for Doug and I, it wasn't over. The old woman who owned the house had now become beside herself with grief and fear. And to make matters worse, she latched onto both of us screaming "VC Cat a Dau!" (cut our throats), and clawing and sobbing at both of us.

Of course her fear was that because the VC soldier had been captured under her house, she and her family would be blamed and they would have their throats cut in retribution. That's how it worked in Vietnam. Makes you wonder who the good guys really were (Not). And so it went on...her family also joined in the carrying-on while Doug and I tried to pack up our kit and move to the next task.

All of a sudden the Grunts turned up and sorted it, rounding them all up as well as the rest of the village, and moved the lot of

55

them to a big cleared area. In minutes, a Chinook Helicopter landed and the lot were herded on board so the old lady got her wish. The village was destroyed and its population relocated to a prepared hamlet in a safe zone where supposedly they could not be gotten at. Doug and I…well, we continued on searching the village finding nothing as exciting as our first house offered up.

From memory, we moved back to Nui Dat…Doug went back to 3 Tp lines and myself back to my tent in 1 Tp lines. A few days later, Doug went home to Australia with his tour complete and I stayed on for many months, as I was just starting my stint. We saw each other again some 45 years later and have been keeping in contact since. I believe Doug received an MID for his efforts and he relates that the most fearsome thing in the whole incident was worrying about me hanging around behind him with a cocked 9-mm pistol.

Hammond M. Salley

Major, US Army, Infantry (Retired)

I arrived in Saigon for my first tour in Vietnam in August 1967 and was assigned to Headquarters, 6th PSYOP Battalion as the Assistant S-3. In December 1967, the 6th Battalion was re-flagged as the 4th PSYOP Group.

On 30 January 1968, the 'TET Offensive' commenced. An eventful situation — especially with all our weapons were under lock and key at the Group Headquarters in Cruz Compound located on Phan Ngu Lao Street and our billets were several miles away. When we dared to return to work and brave the streets, I found a spent bullet lying on the floor of my Quonset hut office.

In February...unbeknownst to me...LTC Beck, the 4th Group CO had provided my name to Military Assistance

Command Studies and Observation Group (MACVSOG) as a candidate to support 'Special Projects' at MACVSOG's Forward Operations Base-3 (FOB-3), Khe Sanh Combat Base. Shortly, I was on my way to 5th Special Forces Group Headquarters in Nha Trang and then much further north.

This was a stimulating assignment to say the least. Turns out that MACVSOG was a Top Secret special operations organization that conducted cross border reconnaissance into Cambodia, Laos and North Vietnam. The Khe Sanh Combat Base was located close to the DMZ and the Laotian border and manned by 5,000 men of the 26th Marine Regiment. FOB-3 was co-located on the periphery of the Combat Base which had already been under siege by 20,000 North Vietnamese regulars as well as constant artillery, rocket and mortar fire for several weeks. My attention was grabbed on the approach to FOB-3 when we were told that due to incoming, the helicopter would not land but that we would have to exit the helicopter by jumping out and running for cover.

Once I managed to find my way to FOB-3's underground bunker, I was informed that all reconnaissance missions and Special Projects were on hold due to the siege. Accordingly, as the Army freely employs the concept of 'extra duties as assigned', I was made the S-2 for the FOB. That opened a window for me as to Top Secret activities in Vietnam and elsewhere about which history books are now written.

All incoming cargo aircraft were called 'rocket magnets' as both a C-123 and a C-130 had been hit and destroyed on the Khe Sanh runway. The constant shelling eventually precluded any normal combat delivery of 'beans and bullets.' Instead, they were now delivered by parachute. The drop zone was just outside the Combat Base wire where Marines had to retrieve the supplies once they hit the ground. Unfortunately, in several cases, it appeared that we also fed NVA troops when some pallets overshot the drop zone.

Our FOB's immediate headquarters was Command and Control North (CCN) located near Marble Mountain in Da Nang. Some of the folks there must have started feeling sorry for us and pieced together a pallet of resupplies for parachute delivery. They stacked cartons of sodas and some booze in the middle of the pallet. Then surrounded those items with C-Ration boxes and other necessities so the sodas couldn't be seen.

Although we were expecting the supplies, we were unaware that CCN was doing something special for us. Another airdrop took place and the supplies were brought back into the Combat Base by the Marines. Later, instead of being notified to come retrieve our supplies, our CO was ordered to report directly to the Marine Base Commander. Turns out that the chute on our pallet didn't open, causing our supplies to be scattered over the drop zone. The Base Commander angrily wanted to know why we were getting sodas and booze when his Marines were only getting beans and bullets. We were apparently wasting valuable airlift cargo space. Gifts of some of the sodas and booze assuaged hard feelings.

Ted Poull, Jr.

Company A, 2d Battalion, 5th Cavalry Regiment, 1st Cavalry Division (Airmobile)
1970

"Remembering Vietnam"

Prologue:

One rocket came in but not too much after that. I had point again on the right file. A claymore mine blew last night. Everyone up all night and scared. John Leatherman is the platoon Sergeant and Karl is squad leader. A 105 mm artillery round came in but did not go off! It could have wiped us all out! Friendly fire screw up! Karl's radio was on, and the music made me home sick.

June 16... Had 1st Light to Fight at 6:30 am. Very spooky and still dark out. Had a Thunder Bolt (a bomb to clear brush for a clearing) at 1:30pm. Raining real hard again! Slept like a log.

June 17... Was out at the C.A. pad by 8:30am. Waited until 4:30 pm to get picked up. We stayed just on the side of the L. Z. for the night. Raining again! Had another cold meal but was hungry so it was good.

June 18...C.A. into an ARVN LZ. I think was called Commer Co. B 2/8 Cav found lots of bicycles, racks of auto and truck parts. (Note these were on huge platforms made of bamboo, together it could be about the size of a large store. Also, we walked in the dark to rescue this platoon. It took us hours to find them, and they were nearly out of ammo). We pushed 1300 meters. I had point again. Co. B 2/8 made contact and we moved up. They had 4 line 2's (wounded). They were only platoon size. The rest of their Co. went back to Vietnam. They did not have OP's (Observation Position) out. They were just sitting around and talking when chi coms, (Chinese grenades) and B-40 rockets hit. They killed two and one got away.

Very flakey night...Could not dig a foxhole. We got there in the dark. I could not see more that four feet in front of me. Karl had no foxhole. Raining hard and getting soaked. Too flakey to even eat last night. Medevac took out the wounded.

Note, that during our rescue of this platoon we got some contact just as I got to the platoon. We had a few wounded and my friend Pete may have been killed. This was a really tough day.

June 19... We moved away from the cache of bikes and auto parts. Karl told me that Pete may have been killed. He got lost and ahead of his squad and seemed like an NVA (or could have been friendly fire). I got the shakes over the news. Pete's squad went out in the 2nd of 8th area and a B-40 rocket hit them, killing one and wounding 6 others. Bad scene! One was hit in the head with a B-40 rocket. We pulled back and called in an air strike. We will go back tomorrow. Scared shitless and lost my watch yesterday.

61

June 20…Had an airstrike called in and then moved down and secured LZ. Found 600 bike tires and enough racks for them as well. We also found kerosene, chains, and pedals. We cut down stuff for an LZ. Had to blow a tree down with C4 (plastic explosives) from my pack and a big bang followed. Got a one day log yesterday. No news about Pete! Hope he is okay.

Thought we had movement, we threw frags (grenades) and that stopped the movement. Found nothing on morning patrol. Had to mix a c-ration and chicken and rice LRP for my only meal. I heard me and Mike Davis and Doc were put in for AC…(Army Commendations with a "V" for valor.) Bob may take over for being log man for Jim Brown in our platoon. Note, we found over 5000 bikes and more truck parts, ammo, gas tanks and food.

June 21…Bad day! Had contact almost all day. 4-6, 4th Platoon killed one NVA coming down the trail. 1-6, 1st Platoon went on Light for Fight patrol and found one hootch and a big hole for a bunker. Had fire fight. NVA threw chi-com, Chinese grenades, and opened up with 30 caliber machine guns. Sure was flakey! We pulled back and called in air strikes. It struck at the wrong place. Had a real flakey night. Everyone in a bad mood! Frag (grenades) went off! Did not sleep well. Supposed to have more troops sent in. No news of Pete!

June 22…Made contact early in the morning. Crawford, point for the 2nd squad, killed one NVA. Got a B-40 rocket, and aK-47 rounds found. A-Company 1/12 (1st of the 112th cavalry) came in today. What a relief to get help! Starting hauling NVA stuff back. A lot of work! Split 1-1 (1st squad of the 1st Platoon.) Some guys here sent to the rear. Karl taking over the platoon. Mike is squad leader. Moved 250 meters and set up in the rain. Two more claymores mines went off last night. 30 Cal. opened up on us at the first light, daybreak. Got a one day log.

June 23…We moved back to the old FOB (Forward Observation Base.) Lots of work moving back. Met Alex from

Basic Training. He's with A_Co. 1/12. Glad to see him alive. We found NVA ruck sacks (packs), gas motors, wielding rods, trailers for trucks, truck parts, about 400 more bikes, wheels and frames for bikes and tires. Also went back to where we first made contact. Felt shaky going back. Picked up some stuff from the guys that got killed. Feel sad picking it up. Battalion sent us ice cream. Tasted good but it was all melted (it was sent in artillery gun powder canisters). We rejoined up with A-Co. 1st/12th and set up with them. Heard Pete might have died. Made me feel sick. We might go in on the 25th.

June 24... We walked west from the other Company. Crossed the road and the Lt. said to "move on." We made contact. Did not find anything but an AK-47 and blood trail. We are all very tired, just no push left in us. Top 1st Sergeant is sick and the Co. and Lt. are also sick. Hope we go in soon, we need a rest. Company Captain, Co. wanted us to keep going. Finally Top found a good place to F.O.B. for the night. Hope we go in soon.

June 25... Humped our asses off today to a clearing to a clearing. Then we CA'd (Combat Assault) with the helicopters to where a battalion size F.O.B. D company found over five million rounds of AK-47, four thousand Chi Coms, 165 SKS rifles, and four miles of communication wire. This find is bigger than "The City," another big cache found and was in the news. Also 400,000 B40 rockets, 2,000 82 mm motor rounds, four thousand 57 mm rounds. The NVA were pissed! Fifty guys were hit trying to get this. From our company one Lt., the Captain and Top went in due to sickness. Karl has the Lt's position and Mike and Dave has what is left of the platoon, our Lt. is company commander. Note, we were down from 120 men to about 50. Karl and Dave are sergeants about my age or younger. Not much was left of our company.

June 26... Finally got CA out of here! We went to LZ Gonder, a special forces camp. Then took a Chinook to Loc Ninh and then Bien Hoa for a battalion stand down. I finally felt relaxed. There was a band playing. I got mail and finally a shower.

They blew that huge cache in place. It made a big bang and blew holes in the ground. I did not recognize most of the guys with clean clothes, haircuts, and shaves. I wish the whole tour were like this.

I heard that Pete and Ken did not make it. I got pretty drunk trying to deal with their deaths.

Epilogue:

When we came into Bien Hoa Air Base the entire airport of people parted to let us through. We were a rough looking bunch. Our clothes were ripped, dirty and blood stained. We all needed shaves and showers. Many had jungle rot on our faces, hands, and feet. It's a condition where the skin cannot stop infection because it is always exposed to wet and dirty conditions. We all had the one-thousand-yard stare from the battles. My rifle was held together by shoestrings which made is hard to shoot but I got it to work. Some guys used shoestrings to tie their pants legs together or tied around the soles of shoes so they could walk. It was 57 days since we had a break like this.

We did get new troops to fill out the Company (about 75 were new and 25 seasoned troops) and we were sent back to Quan Loi three days later. We thought we had dealt a blow to the NVA but on our first patrol on June 29, we were in contact again. This time all the new guys, which was about the majority of the Company, just laid down. The rest of us that had been under fire, battle seasoned, moved up and laid down and fired our weapons. I had to drag the machine gunner and his weapon up to the line because this was his first firefight. Makes me wonder, *was I like these new guys when I first got here?*

I learned a lot in 57 days.

Postscript: In a subsequent exchange of notes via email, Ted shared the following additional comment regarding the huge weapons cache found in Cambodia:

That huge cache we found was so large that when we fob at nite every one was about 4 feet apart so there would be enough me to surround it. This was an entire battalion trying to secure this cache.

It was almost like a downtown area but instead of shops it was bamboo platforms with stuff packed about 6 to 8 foot high in some places.

Grunt Terms:

To help with translation I'm including some short references...

Automatic Ambush — with a battery and clay more mine and trip wire it was made. If someone walked into it they would be blown up. Sometimes we made them with trip wire and grenades.

AO — area of operation

KC — Kit Carson scout. This person was a Montagnard, French for mountain person.

LRP or short for units that were Long Range Patrol. It was also used for the label of freeze-dried food we ate. We stayed in the jungle for 2 weeks or more at a time. "Coming in" to us meant being sent to any open area to help build an LZ or landing zone.

LZ — Landing Zone. It was also where mortar and artillery positions were placed.

CA – Charlie Alpha stood for a helicopter flight. In our case it was a Combat Assault mission.

Kick Out — Sometimes our resupply was done through a chopper just kicking out supplies to us from 150 feet or more above us. This was due to no open space to land a chopper for supplies. There were days when we had not been supplied. We lived on pineapples. The water we drank was from what we caught in our helmets when it rained or bomb craters.

FOB — Forward observation base. It meant we were out in the jungle.

CO — Company commander

LT — lieutenant

Click — A term used to describe 1000 meters

RTO — Radio transmitter operator

Kick Out — When there was no place to land the supplies were kicked out of a chopper which was several hundred feet above us and shove out supplies

1-6 — A reference to each platoon, such as 1-6, 2-6, 3-6 or 3 platoons

Medevac — A chopper which would take out the dead and wounded. Sometimes they could land so cables were used to hoist the wound and dead up to the chopper

Contact — Usually meant a firefight or gun battle

OP — Observation Point

Chicom — A Chinese grenade

Frags — Grenades

C-Rations — Food rations from WW-II

Grunt — A term used to describe people in the infantry.

Marty Hauser
FSB C2, DMZ
April 1970 to Jan. 1971
SP4 and Acting Jack

It was a normal day on FSB C2 in late November 1970. The Top Sergeant came down not my bunker and told me to get my gear together, that I was going home…"The World!"

I couldn't get my stuff together fast enough. All the while, wondering how I was going to say goodbye to the only family I had for a year in a place where I didn't know from one day to the next if I would lose anyone from that small family. So I got my gear and said my good-byes as fast as possible trying not to show any emotion, God forbid that I should let any one of them know exactly what they have meant to me. That would take thirty years later to happen.

No, I'm in that jeep driving own Highway 9 thinking this is the last time I will cross that bridge and go through that village. I'll never again have to worry about driving on that road. Sitting at the small airport at Dong Ha, I start to think about home and how great its going to be to touch my feet on home solid once again and to see Mom and Dad and the family.

It's a long trip home. Had to go all the way back down to Cam Rahn Bay to fly out. But thirty-six hours later, I was in Tacoma, Washington to process out. I got a welcome home steak (if you want to call it a steak) dinner, a couple speeches on going into civilian life, and it was goodbye from the Army.

I set up a flight to Los Angeles, went to the airport, flew into LA, got out of the plane, and it hit me. I just returned from a war and nobody gave a damn...no parades, no thank you, nothing. No one even knew I was coming home. I had to call my Dad at his work to let him know I was at the airport and needed a ride home.

While I was in the airport the unkindly phrases started to flow from the mouths of stupid people. Things like "baby staffer," "village burner," etc...so I tried to stay out of sight and to myself until my ride got there. On the ride home the area seemed like a different world than I remember I only had small talk with my Dad on the way home. After getting settled in I tried to get back into being a civilian again, but no one told me how hard that was going to be. A simple think like getting a job...no work for Vietnam veterans. People didn't seem to want a vet working for them. I guess they thought there must be something wrong with us...we couldn't be normal. So, I found work in a gas station.

I started running around with the wrong people (too young) and started drinking too much. And a couple of times, when I went to gatherings with friends, all they wanted to know was, "How many VC did you kill?" or "Did you collect ears like we heard?" and "Were you always high on drugs?" After a while, it was easier not to let people know that you were a Vietnam veteran.

Slowly, I began to build a wall around myself and didn't want to be around people. My way to hide was to spend a lot of time by myself at the beach just sitting there and trying to figure out why life wasn't like the old days. But I had been to a place that changed my life in a way that made it never the same again.

My days back from Vietnam were spent like this for almost two years after I returned. Then I met my present (my second) and my life started to change very, very slowly. I'm sure, not as fast as she would have liked. She started to bring me out of that shell and started to knock that wall down. It has taken her twenty-eight years of marriage to do that. And, I will never be able to repay her for all the understanding and patience she has had with me. God knows I have her a lot of hell, but she's still here and I thank her for that.

Dan Simpkins
The Royal Australian Regiment (RAR)

**Corporal Ted Collins and Captain Dan
Simpkins: Troop 10, 17th Construction
Squadron - 12/10/1966 - Vang Tau, Vietnam**

"An Australian In Vietnam"

In January 1967, I was given a warning order that I was to take an engineer detachment out on operations under command of D Company, 5RAR. The task of the detachment would be to provide engineering support to the rifle company in the establishment of an outpost position near Dat Do, and to undertake clearing for a proposed barrier minefield. The detachment would take plant items consisting of three International TD15B bulldozers, one Caterpillar 966 front-end loader and one Caterpillar Cat 12 grader, a plant fitter or mechanic, and five field engineers. The total in the detachment was therefore 14 (myself, plant sergeant, field sergeant, plant fitter, five plant operators and five field engineers).

Major Warren Lennon, Officer Commanding 17 Construction Squadron, told me that I could have the pick of any of the members of the squadron — a nice gesture now that I can see it in retrospect. Anyway, I had to take field engineers (who had the same basic training as infantry men, but with specialist engineering skills, including the use of explosives), so I took fellows I knew from my troop, plant operators from Plant Troop and a plant fitter (or mechanic) from the RAEME Workshop. I finished up with myself, Joe Rose, (my troop sergeant from 10 Troop [I asked him if wanted to come out with me, and he said he would not volunteer, but "who the hell is going to look after you if I don't come?"]), a plant sergeant named Bert Warren from Plant Troop (an odd chap from Grafton who used to talk to the items of plant but not to us ["Good morning, Grader – I see you have a flat tyre – I'll get that fixed for you shortly"] that sort of thing), five field engineers from my troop (I can remember the name of only one – Sapper Jackson), five plant operators (again only one I can recall, a Sapper Simpson), and the plant fitter – Craftsman Tommy Goddard. Tom originally came from Alice Springs, and was reputedly the best plant fitter in the squadron, but he had a reputation as a drinker, so I decided to pair him up with me so that I could keep an eye on him.

I handed over my troop, 10 Troop, to an officer newly arrived in Vung Tau, Bruce Kemp — a sad event for me. My troop had arrived in South Vietnam in April 1966. Our corps of engineers had opted for a one-for-one replacement system, as opposed to the infantry system of replacing one complete battalion, or unit, with another, where the bonds formed in training in Australia continued through in actual combat. However, the engineers would not have the benefit of that. The 17th Construction Squadron, as a unit, would remain in South Vietnam for the duration of the war. The members of my troop would go home separately, and not see each other again for years — in my case, not until 1994 when I attended our first reunion in Corowa in Victoria.

The operation in which I and my detachment would be involved, Operation Leeton, was to occupy a hill just north of the town of Dat Do, south east of Nui Dat. This hill was known as "The Horseshoe," so called because of its U shape when viewed on a map. Because Dat Do is in the centre of a rich rice growing area, and was known to be under the influence of the Viet Cong, it was considered that the Horseshoe feature should be permanently occupied by part of the Australian force. The Australian Force Commander, Brigadier Graham, had decreed that a barrier minefield was to be constructed from the Horseshoe southeast to the sea, with the aim of keeping the VC out of the rice bowl area. But the logic was faulty from the very beginning — the VC were known to be in Dat Do, so the VC would be on both sides of the barrier, so how could the barrier minefield keep the VC out of the rice bowl if they were already on both sides? The Horseshoe would provide a base for patrolling and observation. A battery of artillery, 105 mm guns, would be permanently deployed at the Horseshoe, able to provide supporting fire back around the Task Force base at Nui Dat if it came under attack, and also to support patrols and operations originating from the Horseshoe.

The minefield however defies explanation. As any junior officer knows because it is drilled in to them in the teaching establishments, a minefield must be covered by observation and fire. There were insufficient Australian troops in South Vietnam to provide this coverage. Initial planning was that the Australians would patrol the barrier, but even had this been done, a patrol does not constitute the continual observation and coverage by fire that would be required. ARVN outposts were supposed to provide the necessary cover for the minefield, but failed to do so. The barrier minefield became the greatest disaster of the Australian presence in South Vietnam. But that was in the future — we had the task, when the occupation of the Horseshoe was complete, of undertaking the clearing of vegetation along the seven miles, or a little over 11 kilometers, of the path to the sea so that the laying of the mines, a 1 Field Squadron responsibility, could commence.

I was dismayed with the concept of the minefield – I had just finished reading Bernard Fall's book, *Street Without Joy*. (I had bought it in Singapore whilst I was on R & R), in which he described the casualties experienced by the French from mines used by the Viet Minh, many of which had been lifted by the Viet Minh from French installed minefields. And here we were about to do the same thing! One of the principal subjects at Duntroon had been the study of Military History, and it had been impressed on us as cadets that one must learn from the mistakes of the past so that they would not be repeated in the future. So our commanders failed on two counts — failure to obey the military requirement that a minefield must be covered by observation and fire, and failure to learn from a previous military disaster. Sad to say, Bernard Fall was himself killed in Vietnam while on a patrol with US Marines in February 1967.

The occupation of the Horseshoe was entrusted to D Company of 5RAR, under the command of Major Paul Greenhalgh, with an artillery battery and my engineer detachment under command. The deployment plan was that, following an artillery preparation in which the Horseshoe would be plastered with 105 mm shells to help convince any VC that they should vacate the area, the infantry company plus part of the engineer detachment would be inserted by helicopter, and the guns and the engineer plant would be moved from Nui Dat under armored protection when the feature was secured. At that time, the only Australian armor in South Vietnam consisted of APCs. Myself, Sergeant Rose and the sapper field engineers would be part of the helicopter insertion. So those of us to accompany the infantry were at Luscombe Field at Nui Dat before first light and shuffled into "chalks" (if my memory is correct, a "chalk" was six men to a helicopter), and then we just had to wait for the flight of choppers to arrive. It was during this waiting period that another officer came down from 5RAR and told us that Major Bruce McQualter had died of wounds — he had been wounded some days previously in the vicinity of Dat Do — so we knew that it was not going to be a nice place. I had met Bruce in Singapore at the end of my rest and recreation leave (R & R) only a few weeks previously, and the news was hard to take.

The American Hueys arrived like a long line of dragonflies, landed, we got on, and away we went. It is only a short flight from Nui Dat to Dat Do, but it was beautiful to be up in the cool air just as the sun was coming up, and then we landed. There were only a few seconds to get out of the helicopter, with three men going one side and three the other, the chopper was moving away, and the next was coming in. Then I had to get hold of my detachment, as they came in on the following choppers. The company commander wanted me urgently — there must have been something wrong with the ammunition used in the artillery preparation before we came in because there were reports of unexploded shells. The Horseshoe is in fact the remains of a volcano, so it was as hard as the hobs of hell, and there should have been no problems with the detonation of artillery shells. But there had been either a mistake with fuse settings (hard to believe with our gunners following the extremely professional job that had been done with artillery support in the battle of Long Tan), or the shells or fuses were from a faulty batch. No matter that I had been working on buildings, culverts, concrete, etc for the last nine months— now I was to earn my pay in other aspects of military engineering! So Joe, my sergeant, and I commenced that work immediately — I wanted to see how bad these things were before my field engineers got involved. The infantry would mark any unexploded shells (UXBs in Army parlance — Unexploded Bombs) that were found by tying a bit of rag to a nearby bush, so that we would have no trouble in locating the shell, and we blew them in place. I think it took us about three days to blow all the UXBs. A couple we found had the casing split, and the explosive inside was running out the side of the shell with a little column of smoke curling up from it — scary stuff when you are taping some plastic explosive and a detonator to the shell.

The artillery battery was placed in the centre of the Horseshoe, and we were placed on the inside face above the guns. Noisy bastards — they were busy every night. The infantry platoons occupied the high ground above us.

We had two immediate tasks. The first was to clear the outside face of the Horseshoe of all vegetation to provide clear fields of fire in case of attack, and this was a tricky operation. We used the TD15B bulldozers. The outer slope was 45° and our old machines were OK going down, but found the return in reverse very hard, so this task took a little longer than we at first anticipated.

The second task was to construct machine gun bunkers overlooking the external approaches to the feature – one in each of the four platoon areas. (It was a four platoon area. An infantry company has three platoons, so a platoon from another company was rotated out from Nui Dat for a two day stay each to make up the fourth platoon). The Horseshoe is solid rock, so to excavate for the bunkers, which would be made from heavy timber, we had to use explosives. We used popping charges — not big charges, because we wanted to make sure that the rock surrounding the bunker location would not be fragmented. This would cut down the possible effects of loose rock being flung around if the Horseshoe ever came under mortar or artillery fire from the VC. The infantry in the area of the bunker would remove the spoil from the bunker hole after we had detonated our popping charges, and then another round of small holes for the explosives would be drilled, more charges laid, and so on. It was slow work. One morning I was told that in one of these holes, the infantry section had killed a king cobra — a big black snake that measured 16 feet (5 meters). Apparently it had fallen into the pit during the night, and after stand-down in the morning, the diggers had assembled to start cleaning out the spoil from a blast that we had made at last light the night before, and there was this very angry king cobra on the floor of the pit. So they stood and watched it for a while, until one of them said, "Bugger this," leapt into the pit and took the snake's head off with a backhand swing from his entrenching tool. It takes no imagination to realize what would have happened if he had missed! The carcass was hung out on the defensive wire we had out in front of the pits. It was a tourist attraction until it started to stink.

And talking of stink, one morning, early, two APCs barreled into our area and a "gung ho" 2nd Lt leant out and asked if we were the engineers. With the affirmative, the back door of one of the APCs was lowered, and two dead VC that had been killed in an ambush the night before were rolled out, and this little hot shot said, "Bury these for us," and away they went. Bert Warren gave the job to Sapper Simpson (this is why I remember him) and he dug a slot with his dozer, rolled them in and covered them. But in only two days the smell was unbearable, so I told Simpson to dig them out, dig a deep hole, and bury them properly. End of smell.

Another snake story…We always had stand-to in the mornings — deathly quiet, no smoking, waiting for the world to turn grey and then come alight. One morning, just as we stood down, three shots rang out — Blam, blam, blam! Back to the pits — anxious faces. No one knew what was going on. So I sent Tommy Goddard down to the company command post to see what he could find out. He came back with a big grin and told us the story. One of the gunners in the battery below us had been given the job at stand-down to go and light the excess cordite — the guns used bags of cordite depending on the range, and if on short range, as they were at the Horseshoe because our threat was close in, then the excess bags were tossed into a heap in the centre of the battery. Cordite burns in the open — it does not explode. Every morning, the gunners would burn off the excess cordite. On this particular morning, a gunner had gone over to the heap of cordite bags, thrown in a match, and Whoomph, a big mass of flame. Out of the fire came a very angry king cobra — black, hood out, head one meter above the ground — the soldier calmly took the rifle off his shoulder (remember, we carried arms at all times) and fired three quick rounds — all three through the neck just under the head. One dead cobra! What a shot! This snake was a big one too.

We were shelled one evening by the American 155 mm guns, which were located at Nui Dat in support of the Australian Task Force, when they were registering targets. A few rounds landed in the wrong place. A bit scary — that's when Tom reckoned I saved his life. We were sitting on the edge of our pit after stand-down — dark — having a quiet smoke, cupped hands, ensuring no light could be shown. There was an explosion up on the ridge above us, and bits of shrapnel and rock were flying around our ears, and leaves and branches started falling.

Tom leapt to his feet and yelled "Some bastards chucking rocks!" So I hit him behind the knees and he fell back into our firing pit, and I followed him in. We were OK, but Tom reckoned I was the whitest man he knew! He and I got on pretty well, and he didn't get on the grog or play up out at the Horseshoe with me at all.

And another anecdote...The Americans were conducting an operation out to a place called Xuan Moc to the east and they staged through our area. As part of the hands across the sea and us being allies and all, the Americans supplied the fourth platoon for the night they were in our area. Now every morning, Paul Greenhalgh, the Delta Company commander, would have an orders group (O Gp) — himself, his platoon commanders, the company sergeant major (CSM), the mortar fire controller (MFC), the artillery forward observer (FO), me (the engineer) — normal routine. This particular morning, the American platoon commander came down the hill dressed like John Wayne — flak jacket, helmet, crossed bandoliers, a .45 on his hip, carrying an Armalite rifle, grenades hanging everywhere — he looked like the Hollywood version of American fighting men. "Say guys, do ya know where I can find the Company Commander?" We all were standing in a rough circle, with bush hats, jungle greens and boots, all of us carrying rifles. Paul said, "That's me." The John Wayne look-a-like stood to attention and threw an almighty salute — it was beautiful, but Paul said, very quietly, "We don't salute in the bush". Anyway, the John Wayne impersonator thanked Paul most profusely for providing such a good billet. I heard later in the day that the Americans had used the firing pits as latrines and had shit in nearly every one. We were not impressed.

An infantry platoon commander, 2nd Lt Mick Deak, from D. Company 5RAR, conducted an exemplary action just out in front of the Horseshoe. He took out an ambush patrol of about eight men, and savaged a VC company. One of his fellows took a machine gun round through his lower leg that blew the bone out — they got him out by medevac helicopter under fire. About 30 VC were killed from a combination of small arms fire from the ambush, and artillery and mortars controlled by Mick. We watched the fireworks from up on the hill. Mick Deak had already been decorated with a Military Cross for an action in September 1966. It is interesting that another platoon commander in D Company, Dennis Rainer, had also been awarded the same decoration.

The company second in command (2IC) was a chap named Fred Pfitzener who was two years ahead of me in seniority from Duntroon, but he was located back in Nui Dat, and looked after re-supply for those on the Horseshoe. But Fred spent one night out on the Horseshoe. He had smuggled some beer out with him, and Joe Rose (my sergeant) and I were invited to share a cold one. We joined Fred and the CSM in the clump of bamboo near our pit, and we settled down for a yarn and a beer. We had probably only had one each, when the snapping of twigs and rattle of stones alerted us that someone was trying to join us. A figure appeared in the gloom, in full battle array, and rifle, and demanded to know who we were and what were we doing. Fred must have recognized him, and told him to "piss off!" When sanity returned, Fred explained that he was a CMF (Army Reserve) officer, a major, from Tasmania who had scored a visit to Vietnam — a policy introduced to give some experience to army reservists, even if the visits only lasted two weeks. I realized years later when I was posted to Tasmania, from the name of the lieutenant colonel commanding a reserve infantry battalion that he was the same chap from the Horseshoe.

Another night there was action away to the southeast of the Horseshoe. The crump of artillery and mortars, the bark of machine gun fire, flares, tracers — all the panoply of war. But the *piece de resistance* was without the doubt the finale. We could hear the dull sound of aircraft engines, which one of our group recognized as those from a DC3. Then there was an incredible beam of light emanating from a point in the sky, following a wavy path to the ground, where it spattered and scattered and broke up in all directions, followed by a noise that could only be likened to a giant ripping a gigantic sheet of canvas. This was "Puff the Magic Dragon," an American machine gun mounted in the fuselage of an old DC3, firing at an incredible rate of 6,000 rounds per minute, and the light we were watching was made up of the tracer rounds, so quickly following each other that it became a continuous beam of light. If it was awe inspiring to us, imagine how the VC would feel being subjected to that incredible example of firepower.

The order was given to start clearing the alignment from the Horseshoe down to the sea for the barrier minefield. Another complete infantry company had the job of building the barbed wire fence that would enclose the minefield, and to provide protection to the dozers doing the clearing. My detachment was not involved in mine laying — but we did the clearing.

Tommy Goddard, the plant fitter, would make a daily run along the cleared zone to where the dozers were working for refueling, servicing and maintenance of the machines. Once, when I travelled with Tom, we stopped near the headquarters element of the infantry company providing security to the dozers doing the clearing. I went over and introduced myself to Major Ron Shambrook, the infantry company commander responsible for the protection of our machines. He told me that a sniper had been active that morning back towards the Horseshoe. I told Tom as we set out to drive back to the Horseshoe — he was driving — and I reckon that Land rover did 80 miles an hour, on a rough track, with the trailer airborne more often than with its wheels in contact with the ground! I remember Tom saying, "That fucking sniper will have to work hard to get us, boss!" And I was in no mood to disagree.

There was a daily supply run from the Task Force base at Nui Dat — helicopters would bring in rations and water. For some unaccountable reason, we were on American ration packs — the only good things in them as far as I was concerned were a small packet of cigarettes and a can of fruit. I lived on the fruit — I could not eat the other items. (On my return to Australia, because I had lost a lot of weight, I was described as a greyhound — "all prick and ribs!") Water also was delivered in plastic jerry cans, because we had no water point at that stage. A well boring machine from our parent unit was sent out to the Horseshoe, an engineer item of plant under the control of WO Kev Rapley, who was the Plant Warrant Officer in 17 Construction Squadron, but in my time on that feature, the boring was not successful. But Kev managed one good deed — he smuggled some beer out to us when he brought the well boring machine to the Horseshoe.

We arranged for our sappers to get back into Nui Dat for a clean-up (no showers on the Horseshoe) after a few weeks. I managed to get back to Nui Dat only once in my time on the Horseshoe, and it was a trip that lives in my memory. The RAAF considered that helicopter flying was safe if you were above 3,000 feet, or if you were flying at ground level. For my trip, the super stud pilot reckoned that it was safer to fly on the deck, and he was so low that the chopper had to jump up to rise over the paddy bunds. My adrenalin level was very high. I remember thinking that if the pilot misjudged our height above ground level, the skids underneath the chopper would catch on a bund and we would cartwheel across the paddy, but he obviously knew what he was doing. We landed at Nui Dat in the late afternoon — there was some entertainment group up from Australia, and the only thing I can remember was the female singer Noeline Battly, who sang "Tar and Cement". And it was the first shower that I had had in about two weeks. My clothes were filthy — so was I. And the next morning back to the war.

I was out on the Horseshoe until about four days before I finally departed to Australia in April. I handed over command of the detachment to Mick Tarte, another classmate of mine from Duntroon, and a recent arrival in South Vietnam. He came out on a helicopter with some other replacements. The helicopter was supposed to wait for me, but by the time I had shown Mick what was what, and introduced him to the fellows who were staying (some were to go back with me), the helicopter had gone. 1 Field Squadron had one low loader, 17 Construction Squadron had another, both old 1941 Federals, and one of these had brought out a repaired dozer from Nui Dat that afternoon. The corporal driving it said he was not going to stay the night at the Horseshoe, and if we wanted to, we could ride with him. So about four of us settled on the trailer — the driver and his offsider were in the cab. The offsider stood on his seat with his head and shoulders out of the hatch in the cabin roof manning a machine gun. We arranged some sandbags on the deck of the trailer to give us some form of protection. No escort — it was bloody stupid I suppose. But away we went, through Dat Do to Baria and up to Nui Dat, no problems...after dark, too!

And when we got back to Nui Dat, I had two beers, and promptly went to sleep. I was camped in a tent that belonged to another officer who was out on an operation — there was another fellow in the tent, but I took no notice — I was exhausted. About 3 am I heard the cough of some mortars (we had heard them frequently on the Horseshoe), and I was out of the cot into the pit in no time flat. Practice I suppose. I could hear the other poor chap scrabbling around in the tent trying to find his boots, his weapon, swearing, but finally he fell into the pit. No worries — the VC threw a few mortars on the American 155s, not on us.

The next morning, Gerry Stapleton, the captain in charge of the I Field Squadron Workshop (RAEME), whose nickname was "Shacklefoot," said that he wanted a day away after the previous night's activity, and offered me a lift to Vung Tau, which I accepted, together with my soldiers from the Horseshoe. When we arrived in Vung Tau, we bought a carton of beer and headed for the beach. Scratch one day. I spent only another few days in Vung Tau, getting organized for my return. Because I would be on civilian aircraft, I had to get a passport, and so my first ever passport was issued by the Australian Embassy in Saigon. But of course, my return could not be straightforward. I was supposed to get a seat on the late afternoon "Wallaby Flight," a RAAF Caribou service from Vung Tau to Saigon, but when I got to the airstrip, I was told the aircraft was grounded. The RAAF chap I spoke to suggested that I try with the Americans — they usually had flights at all times to Saigon. No problems — I could travel to Saigon on a C-123.

I waved goodbye to my escort from the squadron, and scrambled on board. There were no seats — there were a few big boxes in the aircraft hold, and the round portholes were minus glass. A big American sergeant came back and gave me a safety briefing ("If we go down, just get the fuck out of the aircraft") and we took off. The wind howled through the hold, and I watched a large oil slick on one wing as it wriggled first one way and then another.

But we landed at Tan Son Nhut, and then I had to find a friendly Australian to get me into the city and find a bed. Finally, I made it back out to the airport in the morning, and climbed on board a Pan Am flight to Singapore, the only passenger in First Class with two beautiful hostesses to look after me, and then on a Swissair flight to Sydney via Perth.

The Vietnamese people impressed me, not that I had had much contact with them, in their stoic acceptance of a war thrust upon them and the foreigners who had arrived in their midst. It depressed me that the racial slurs of "gooks" "slant-eyes" and "slopes" were in common usage. After all, were we not in this country to help them beat the menace of communism? But worse was the realization that the South Vietnamese government was corrupt and inefficient. I had had very little contact with Americans, but the overall impression was that whilst their equipment generally was superior to ours, their training and performance was of a lower standard.

Explanatory Notes:
The Australian Task Force was based at Nui Dat, north of Baria, in Phouc Tuy Province, north east of Saigon, in III Corps. Initially, there were two infantry battalions in the Task Force, supported by a regiment of artillery (three batteries to a regiment - two Australian and one New Zealand — six 105 mm guns to each battery), a field squadron of engineers, an APC squadron.

The construction squadron was based at Vung Tau.

A squadron is equivalent to a company in infantry terms.
The 'platoon' in a squadron is called a troop.

RAR – Royal Australian Regiment

5RAR – Fifth Battalion, Royal Australian Regiment

RAE – Royal Australian Engineers

RAEME – Royal Australian Electrical and Mechanical Engineers

RAAF – Royal Australian Air Force

CMF – Citizen Military Forces

WO – Warrant Officer

Personal Details:
Graduated from the Royal Military College, Duntroon, in December 1963, with the rank of Lieutenant, allocated to RAE.

Arrived in Vietnam in April 1966 – departed April 1967. Posted to 17 Construction Squadron.

Located on "The Horseshoe" from February to April 1967. My rank in Vietnam was Captain.

Marc R. Perry
101st Airborne Division, Vietnam

"Truth is sometimes stranger than fiction!"

I was born July 4, 1949, in Ferndale, Michigan, and graduated from Ferndale High School in 1967 and soon began a Tool & Die apprenticeship.

I received my draft notice to report to the VFW American Legion Hall in Berkley, Michigan on March 3, 1969, for induction. I joined about 200 other draftees from southeast Michigan and headed to Fort Knox, Kentucky, for two months of Basic Training with Bravo Company in the 11th Battalion of the 4th Training Brigade.

I scored well on the Army's skill tests and was assigned to be a Machinist. As fate would have it, at that time the Army didn't need machinists. Instead, it needed specialists for Armor (tanks), artillery, truck drivers, cooks and record clerks. Since I had learned how to type in high school this was apparently the deciding factor because when the dust had settled, I was assigned as a legal clerk to manage the 4th Army personnel records at Fort Hood near Killeen, Texas. This change of course meant I never received Infantry or Airborne training.

At Fort Hood, I received a Secret clearance in order to work with the legal records and I demonstrated organizational and clerical skills; streamlining the records maintenance process and received two promotions in rapid succession to support my increasing responsibilities. I also performed follow-up investigations of soldiers who'd been incarcerated for various infractions. My efforts resulted in several being exonerated and released — something I doubt would have occurred absent my efforts.

On May 15, 1970, as a Specialist, E4 I finally arrived in Vietnam. My new home was the Phu Bai Combat Base Defense near Hue, 30 miles south of the DMZ where like my father and brother, I was assigned to the 101st Airborne Division. My unit loaned me to the operational command staff of the Northern I Corps, the Headquarters for the entire northern area of Vietnam. I was now an Operations Specialist and one of only two enlisted men on the command staff which had one Lieutenant Colonel, one Major, four Captains and a handful of 1st and 2nd Lieutenants.

Our job was to receive and track the daily reports from all the units in the Northern I Corps. Our "office" was an underground bunker beneath the main HQ building, located in the approximate center of the large base and protected by concrete barriers and sandbags. The base perimeter consisted of barbed-wire fences, trenches, land mines, and 16 guard towers.

Each day, the morning reports updated the current locations and status of all companies and platoons under our command which we tracked on a large wall map. Daily paperwork included target (status) reports, target requests, Close Air Support requests, and rescues. We also tracked casualties and action reports. My immediate boss was Captain Brantley, whom I admired and greatly respected.

The base came under frequent attack from Viet Cong mortars and snipers. Our sleeping "hooches" were sometimes casualties of these attacks. The workers on base were Vietnamese, and it was almost impossible to keep out spies. Luckily there were no perimeter breaks during my nine months I was stationed in Phu Bai Combat Base Defense.

My life was fast-paced and exciting for a "young and immortal" 21-year-old. Sometimes it "felt like I was in a movie" with almost-daily helicopter flights out to the other bases for investigations and inspections. We even inspected some of the South Vietnamese Army (ARVN) bases.

One day while walking through the camp a couple months after my arrival, I noticed a low mound with padlocked doors that looked like a tornado shelter. I discovered that no one, all the way up to the Base Commander, knew its purpose. So Captain Brantley ordered the padlock cut and the doors opened. Inside we found a poorly lit stairway leading down into an underground bunker that contained boxes and boxes of emergency ammunition, M-16 rifles, M-60 machine guns and M-79 grenade launchers that were originally stashed there for use if the base was overrun. Obviously, it had not been or the bunker would most likely been empty.

The base had been originally built by the Marines. Apparently at some point over the years, the turnover briefing between the Base Commander and his successor had neglected to mention the weapons stash. Now we had a problem. No one knew exactly how long everything had been underground, subject to dampness and rust. Would they still function reliably? Rather than take the chance, the Army decided to destroy everything or at least expend it for practice and training rather than distributing it to the front-line troops. Probably a smart decision considering the M-16's later and well-deserved reputation for jamming.

I along with SP4 Robert Brandt, SP4 Jim Eley, SP4 Gene Perry and SP4 Kenny Smith drove to Camp Eagle, home of the 101st Airborne Airmobile not too far from Phu Bai Combat Base Defense.

There along with about 20 infantry we proceeded to target practice and dispense all the ammo that we had found in the underground bunker. Afterwards all of the weapons we had found were cut up and destroyed. For me it was unbelievable that the Army would not have found a better use of the arms, but considering they had been in a damp underground bunker for who knows how long, it was better to destroy them then to have them fail out in the field.

My nine months at Phu Bai were busy and passed quickly. A final highlight occurred in December 1970 when Captain Brantley got us passes to attend the Bob Hope Special at nearby Camp Eagle. It was welcome relief from the daily grind of war. Just two months later, on February 23, 1971, I was honorably discharged from the Army. I was awarded a Bronze Star in recognition of my service and returned home to Michigan, 23 months and 3 weeks after my departure. Like my grandfather, father, and older brother, I had survived a war and now at age 21, I was ready for whatever came next...but that's a story for another time!

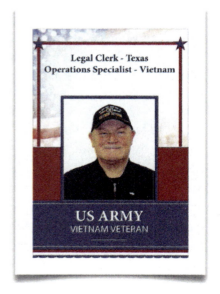

Legal Clerk - Texas
Operations Specialist - Vietnam

US ARMY
VIETNAM VETERAN

John Anders Lindblom
6th Psychological Operations Battalion, 4th Psychological Operations Group

"Reflections"

Prologue:

When I graduated from Albion College in Michigan in 1966, the last thing I wanted to do was get drafted into the Army. The war in Vietnam was raging and the anti war demonstrations across the US were loud and violent. To maintain my academic draft deferment, I applied and was accepted into a graduate masters program at Western Michigan University in Kalamazoo. Although it was an interesting program, and I did well academically, I never took for granted that the real reason I was there was to avoid the draft!

By the time the summer of 1967 arrived, I was starting to experience academic fatigue. After all, I'd been attending school now for 18 years of my life. As the summer quarter arrived, I had a serious girl friend. I was playing music with a group of friends. And there were lots of incredible parties. To enjoy life even better, my room mate and I moved from Kalamazoo city to a small quiet lakeside cabin in the countryside. It was the best summer of my life. However, to fully enjoy it, I enrolled in fewer classes and hence fewer academic credits that academic quarter. As it turned out, those fewer academic credits were below the threshold required by the draft board to maintain the draft deferment.

I received my first draft notice in early May. It came from the Illinois draft board where I was registered, as Illinois was my official home. However, it gave me an opportunity to contest it, which I did, saying that I had lived in Michigan attending school now going on five years. I now considered myself a Michigan resident. Amazingly the Illinois board approved my position and withdrew the draft notice. However, it told me that I would be receiving another notice as soon as the transfer was received by the Michigan draft board. Indeed I received that notice 2 weeks later.

The last thing I wanted was to be drafted. If I had to go into military service, I wanted to be in a position where I could make choices of my own impacting on that experience. So, I started talking to recruiters...Navy, Air Force and Army. I took entry tests. But the time was running out. I had only a few weeks left before I had to go into basic training. The best option I had was offered by the Army recruiter.

The Army was desperate for officers. So they created a 120 day delayed enlistment program if you signed up for Officer Candidate School (OCS). That meant that if I signed up, took all the tests and was accepted, I wouldn't have to physically start training for 4 months. That would give me the rest of the summer and some of the fall to prepare and continue enjoying what had been the best summer of my life. The catch was…I'd be signing up for a 7 year obligation with 3 years on active duty! Well, I thought by the time I finished all the training, maybe the war in Vietnam would be over. I left for basic training the end of September.

One of the major issues with the "draft" was that so many young draftees ended up being sent to Vietnam with only a few months training. They were hardly prepared for the life changing experience they were to encounter in Vietnam. My training lasted more than a year…8 weeks "basic" at Fort Leonard Wood Missouri, 8 weeks AIT at Fort Sill Oklahoma, 6 months OCS also at Fort Sill, 6 weeks Civil Affairs training at Fort Gordon Georgia and 3 months PSYOPs training at the US Special Warfare Center at Fort Bragg. When I left for Vietnam in January 1969, I was very well prepared.

Upon arrival in Vietnam I reported to the 4th PSYOP Group in Saigon where I was processed in and assigned to the 6th PSYOPS Battalion in Bien Hoa. There I went through an introductory orientation process and was eventually assigned a field team consisting of an American staff sergeant and a Vietnamese interpreter. We were further attached to the 3rd Brigade of the 1st Air Calvary Division based in Bing Long Province, a province west of Saigon on the Cambodian boarder. Although we did some arial loudspeaker missions in support of the 1st Air Cav troops, our real work was on the ground interacting with the Vietnamese in support of their activities in the villages and hamlets in the local district. This brought us in close contact with the provincial MACV advisory team and their Vietnamese counterparts. Consequently, it made sense that we be further seconded to the MACV team and allowed to relocate to their compound.

Working with the Vietnamese was an extremely interesting and rewarding cultural experience. It gave us an incredible first hand insight into the tragic impact the war had on the country and its people. Many of the villages we operated in were considered "contested," and even the village and hamlet officials were afraid to spend the night in their own homes for fear of VC nightly incursions and retaliation. Our effort was to support them, give the villagers confidence in their government and attempt to convince local VC gorillas to abandon the communist influence and pressure and return home to support their families and the South Vietnamese government.

However, when the 1st Air Cav needed us to support their operations, they ordered us back. That usually meant that there was field mission in the planning. In April that field mission was Operation Montana Raider.

Operation Montana Raider:
Operation Montana Raider was a coordinated search and destroy operation comprised of the 1st Air Cavalry Division and the 11th Armored Cavalry Regiment along the Vietnam/ Cambodian border in Tay Ninh and Binh Long Provinces of military Corps III. It's objective was to destroy NVA encampments along that border and obtain intelligence on NVA operations in the area, including the possible location of COSVN headquarters (the communist headquarters understood to be coordinating the NVA military operations in South Vietnam). The operation was conducted from April 12, 1969, to May 14, 1969, approximately one month.

Our team consisting of Staff SGT Larry West, SGT Dao Tien Tu (our interpreter) and I were involved in both phases of the operation, being evacuated to the 6th PSYOPS Battalion HQ in Bien Hoa for two days for resupply and briefing before rejoining Phase 2 of the operation. At that time SGT Tu was reassigned to another team to assist in another area of operations. SGT West and I were assigned a "Kit Carson Scout" (an enemy soldier who had defected to the South Vietnamese government) to replace Tu. This new team configuration was in place for the rest of the operation.

Our enemy encounter on April 17 was the most significant battle we were involved with during Phase 1. It involved assaulting an enemy bunker complex on the boarder with Cambodia. Our team was riding on an armored personnel carrier (APC) of G Troop of the 11th ACV when a 1st Air Cav infantry soldier threw a grenade into an enemy bunker we were currently running over. Unfortunately the grenade didn't go into the opening of the bunker and exploded on the side of our APC. The M-60 machine gunner sitting next to me on that side of the APC was literally "peppered" with shell fragments from that grenade. We had to retreat from the action to extract the gunner and get him safely to an evacuation area for medevac. Our APC then returned to the line of battle.

We were immediately under fire. At this time I noticed among the noise, commotion and tracer rounds firing everywhere that an NVA tracer was heading in my direction but then disappeared. (NVA tracers were green in color.) The noise and chaos were so intense that I never realized that I had been hit. SGT West and SGT Tu noticed the blood on my arm. I felt nothing. I noticed that a hole was burning into my flak jacket and that there were fragments in my arm. I was able to pull the fragments out and the kevlar in the flak jacket eventually stopped burning. About the same time we were alerted that one of the bunkers had put up a white flag of surrender. We immediately went to that location. The After Action Report details what happened next.

93

After Action Report:

"Approximately at 1700 we saw a white flag appear from one of the bunkers. This drew not only the attention of our team, but also of the infantry. It was all we could do to keep them from firing into the bunker. My interpreter rushed over to the bunker opening and began to call the occupants out. Meanwhile my sergeant and myself kept all the other troops out of the immediate area for it worried me that the aggressiveness of the troops might accidentally set off a gun battle catching my interpreter in the middle. Three Viet Cong POWs came out almost immediately. They said that there were three more inside but that they would not come out. In fact they told us to go ahead and blow up the bunker. My interpreter tried to get one of the POWs to talk to his comrades inside, but he refused. Consequently, my interpreter risked his life by going right up to the bunker opening and with a small bull horn he talked into the bunker. The rest of my team covered him from behind and from the roof of the bunker. Meanwhile, all around US troops were taking fire and casualties. After approximately 20 minutes of talking and much patience on the part of everybody, we gave the occupants 2 minutes to surrender and come out, or we would blow them up. After a minute of waiting, they came out. They were NVA! One was the group's political officer!!"

What the After Action Report doesn't detail is that after we captured the POWs and the battle was concluded, I had a chance to examine my "wounds." I wasn't bleeding any more, but the hole in my flak jacket made me realize how lucky I was. I'm sure it came from that tracer I saw heading toward me then disappear. It must have hit something in the path of trajectory…a plant or something. Also I had just put on that flak jacket moments before because of the intensity of fire we were about to encounter.

When the battle was over and casualties were being recorded, a Master Sergeant from the 1st Air Cav came over to our

APC. He was looking for me. I was on his list for a Purple Heart. He was not impressed that I wasn't visibly wounded. I also knew that I was incredibly lucky. I told him to remove my name from the list. He happily agreed. Technically I could have received the medal. I figured worse things were going to happen in the future, and when it did, the medal would mean much more. I also remembered the M60 machine gunner who had to be medevaced with serious wounds received from a "friendly" grenade. In those days there were no medals for being wounded by friendly fire. He would get nothing for his wounds!!

Little contact was made in the second phase of the operation. That phase actually took us briefly across the boarder into Cambodia. Cambodia was internationally considered a sovereign country, and incursions into that country were prohibited. But defining exactly where boarders were in this jungle environment was difficult. Fortunately we didn't encounter any enemy during the time we were there and left within a couple of hours back to what we were sure was Vietnam.

Our POWs were airlifted back to the 1st Air Cav's base headquarters for interrogation. From those interrogations it was concluded that most of the enemy bunker locations had been destroyed and COSVN headquarters did not exist in that area of Vietnam. Operation Montana Raider stood down, and all participating forces returned to their respective headquarters.

Operation Minh Duc:

In the months that followed we were relocated a number of times, as the 1st Air Cav brigade moved position around Vietnam's Military Corps III. We worked in the villages and hamlets with local Vietnamese counterparts wherever possible. However, we were never in a location long enough to achieve any significant impact. Whenever we were finally able to gain the trust and

95

confidence of the local authorities and population, the Cav moved to another province. However in the fall of 1969 the 3rd Brigade moved back to Bing Long Province, and we were able to reunite with our colleagues at MACV Team 47 and our Vietnamese counterparts.

Minh Duc village was located in the middle of the Michelin rubber plantation in Binh Long Province and was heavily contested with what was a significant Viet Cong infrastructure. Although there was a South Vietnamese Regional Force troop encampment nearby, it wasn't adequate enough to protect the the village from nightly incursions by the VC. However considering the economic importance of the rubber grown there, it was a key target of the South Vietnamese intelligence and information officials, the local CIA's field unit and our PSYOPS operations. What was significant about this operation was the confirmation that given adequate time in an area, we could actually achieve measurable positive results. Operations in Minh Duc began in early October, 1969.

After Action Report:

Operations in Minh Duc were particularly rewarding this month. As was previously reported, last month our activities concentrated somewhat on this village. In five visits last month our operations initiated counter-propaganda visits by the local VC forces after each visit. Early this month brought the start of the fall of the local VC infrastructure with the rallying of the local VC security chief. On 23 November, our team was called to Minh Duc by CIA's Provincial Recon Unit (PRU), which had received information that there were a number of people in Minh Duc who wished to Chieu Hoi. At the conclusion of about 24 hours on our loud speakers, eleven had rallied. They were all women, members of the local VC women's club.

On the following day we went back accompanied by the Cultural Drama Team. We acquired an additional rallier on that occasion, a 16-year-old boy who said he was part of a VC cultural drama team. He gave us four more names, two women and two boys, who also wished to rally. We went back on the following day and picked these people up. In 3 days we had accounted for 16 Hoi Chanhs from Minh Duc. In my 10 months as a PSYOPS HE team leader, this is the first time I have ever had anyone Chieu Hoi to our truck. This is particularly rewarding since this is the first concrete feedback we've received of the work we've been doing. I feel that the primary reason for this feedback was the fact that our team was finally allowed to stay in one place long enough to follow through on a mission. We have been in Binh Long Province 2 months now and that is the longest we've ever stayed in one place at one time. This should add further credibility to the suggestion that HE field teams be attached to one province and remain there.

On 12 November, our combined team received one hostile incoming round, possibly a B-40, which landed 100 meters from our location during an afternoon drama team performance at Phu Hieng. This, along with the Hoi Chanhs at Minh Duc clearly indicates that the work our team is doing is affective. It is apparent that the enemy knows we exist and has found it important enough to counter our activities.

Epilogue:

As previously alluded to, Vietnam was a life-changing experience for all of us who served. For many, unfortunately, the experience wasn't a good one, and after all these years I personally know some who still suffer from PTSD. As mentioned earlier, I was lucky to have undergone more than one year of training to prepare me for the experience. Ultimately I fell in love with Vietnam and its people. When my 3 year active duty obligation with the Army was completed, I could have continued on active duty, as my overall obligation was 7 years. But I chose instead to go into the State Department's CORDS program where I felt I could have a greater impact. So, I went through more training in Washington DC, including Vietnamese language training. I returned to Vietnam in January 1972, assigned to a MACV advisory team in Pleiku in Central Highlands for 2 more years. By that time all American military forces had left the country for the exception of the MACV advisors and the US Special Forces.

The Spring of 1972 brought an intense North Vietnamese invasion during which South Vietnam lost significant areas in its border provinces with Laos and Cambodia. It was a major test of the South Vietnamese army, and the ARVN didn't measure up to the challenge. Luckily we still had the US 5th Special Forces in our area of the highlands to protect us (...along with B-52s). Special Forces team B-50 was relocated from Ban Me Thuot to Pleiku to secure our area. It was during this time that I met a Vietnamese Special Forces nurse assigned to that team. We fell in love and got married at the end of 1973. (We celebrated our 50th wedding anniversary in December 2023.)

The Vietnam experience also resulted in me spending the rest of my professional career living and working in Asia. My wife and I lived in Singapore for 36 years where we raised our family. Mine was a regional position, so I traveled extensively throughout

Asia. The thrill was when Vietnam opened up in the early nineties, and we were able travel freely there and bond with my wife's family. Eventually I was able to establish an office in Hanoi for the US agricultural organization with which I was working. Vietnam ultimately became one of our largest customers in SE Asia.

On a final note...On one business trip to Vietnam in the mid nineties, I was traveling by road to Can Tho for a meeting. I had made this trip several times, and in Tien Giang Province there was a sign on the road and an arrow pointing to the hamlet of Ap Bac. Ap Bac was the location in 1963 where American advisors and the ARVN went into battle with the Viet Cong and were essentially defeated and had to retreat. Several US helicopters were shot down. The incident was the first time the American Embassy and military advisors realized that the VC weren't just a group of ragtag gorillas. They were a well trained, well armed, dedicated army. I had studied about Ap Bac when in Washington training for the CORDS program. Several books were written about this early turning point event in which John Paul Vann was the lead US military advisor on the ground at the time. (I worked under Vann when I was with CORDS in Pleiku years later.) So, I wanted to stop by and see for myself where this historic battle took place.

When we reached the end of the dirt road to Ap Bac, there was a place to park. The entire area was surrounded by rice paddies. We got out of the car and looked around but could see no evidence of a village or a memorial. There were some villagers walking up the road carrying groceries. They were returning from a nearby market. We asked them about Ap Bac. They knew nothing. One said that there was an "old" man back at the market who might know. I figured the, "old" man was probably my age. But one person in the group did remember seeing some sort of memorial way back in the paddy land. So, we walked the paddy dikes for about a mile or two, with "me" telling those around us the story of the Battle of Ap Bac. We finally found the memorial where the hamlet had been and where the 3 Viet Cong who died during the battle were remembered.

The significance of this experience to me was, that it was clear that the younger generation in Vietnam had moved on. They had no interest in learning the history of the war. The war to them was ancient history. They were focused on the current events, Vietnam's growing economy and the happy satisfaction of today's every day life. I immediately thought if these people can move on why can't we in America. It was so sad that many US veterans still couldn't do the same.

6th PYSOP Team - Bing Long, 1969:
Sgt. Tu / Sgt. Larry West / and myself,
John Anders Lindblom

Chad Spawr
US Army, Vietnam October 1967 - July 1969
1st Infantry Division
MACV Advisory Team 47
6th PSYOP Battalion
2d Brigade 1st Cavalry Division (Airmobile)

Pilot / Chad Spawr / Howard Patrick

"Where Did Those Guys Come From?"

I think we'd all heard about "spooks" and "spies" from the CIA or some other lettered-agency doing their operations in Vietnam, but most of us only heard rumors, never saw anything resembling James Bond or any other "super spy" while we were in country. That all changed one strange day in late 1968.

As the PSYOP team leader for 2d Brigade of the 1st Cavalry Division (Airmobile), I worked with several different maneuver battalions throughout the Brigade's Area of Operations

(AO). Our primary targets were small groups of "local" Viet Cong guerrillas as well as units of the regular North Vietnamese Army (NVA) who were located throughout that part of the country under 1st Cavalry influence.

Since the end of the 1968 Tet Offensive, the VC were reduced to small bands of local guerrillas, certainly nowhere near the well-formed and trained combat units they had been before they were wiped out in battle with Allied forces. My own belief is that the North Vietnamese deliberately put the VC main force units at the "point of the spear" of combat operations for Tet so they'd be largely destroyed and therefore unable to contest the eventual triumph of the North at the future war's end. Just my theory.

Most of our contacts were therefore NVA units, and they were very good soldiers. Well-trained and disciplined, they were tough fighters. While I did not like them personally, I respected their ability to fight hard and inflict casualties on our own forces. That being said, however, there was still a guerrilla presence, and they were always a threat to small unit actions as well as being able to continue a terror campaign against recalcitrant local villagers and government officials.

One of the functions of the PSYOP units was to conduct "movie nights" and a variety of social functions for local villagers to support the legitimate government, convey patriotic messages and themes, and generally promote loyalty to the government and opposition to the communists. There is nothing new about this, and it has been a function in war for centuries. In Vietnam, we called it "winning hearts and minds."

Many of our PSYOP teams operated from vehicles known as "MSQ-85's," a ¾ ton truck with a large container box in place of the rear bench seats. This box contained all manner of audio-

102

visual equipment, a small gas-powered generator to provide electricity to run projectors, loudspeakers, and other powered-equipment. The vehicles were cumbersome and did not like the rough rural environment of a jungled country with no paved roads. Still, they were basically useful for the tasks assigned to the PSYOP units.

While working with a joint cavalry-armor unit near a small village north and west of An Loc, my interpreter and I joined the line of US troops sealing off the village so there was no way for anybody to escape. The plan was to close the seal, and then conduct a thorough search of the village and its inhabitants looking for weapons, any contraband, or any VC and NVA soldiers hiding among the population. We began contracting the seal around 0600 hours. All the villagers were moved to the center of the village, and the search began.

The search was peaceful, but suddenly it erupted in turmoil at one edge of the open square. The Cavalry soldiers brought forward two white men in civilian clothes, both with rucksacks, and carrying AK-47 rifles. When I first saw them, I thought they were the Russians we had heard were advising the communists, but after a few minutes, we learned that they were two CIA officers who had been working with some local villagers who had wanted to surrender (Chieu Hoi) to the government side. As we questioned the two CIA men, we were spooked that they had entered the village during the night while we had it "sealed." Clearly, we didn't.

The excitement was temporary, and the search process yielded no significant results. There were no weapons found, and no VC suspects detained. It was also clear that the villagers were very unhappy to be so disrupted. I decided to break out the film projector and a couple of Vietnamese language films to play for the village. One of the films was a comedy (somehow seemed appropriate at the moment!), and that helped to break the tension between the troops and the villagers. When it was done, we packed up and headed out, taking the two CIA officers with us and dropping them off in An Loc.

I never heard more about that incident, and when I later asked our Intel and Operations officers about it, they just looked at me with that, "Shut up and don't ask questions," stare.

I got the message.

Footnote: A few months later, we saw the direct result of how irritated we had made the communists, when an MSQ-85 was towed into our 6th Battalion HQ with its cab destroyed by a large explosion. The PSYOP team had been showing films in a village when at least one VC cadre tossed a satchel charge into the cab. The explosion destroyed the entire cab, set the interior on fire, and rendered it totally inoperable. It was a sobering reminder of just how vulnerable a PSYOP team could be in conducting its missions in a "hot" combat zone.

In the company of CIA

Stanley Michelsen
7th PSYOP Battalion
4th PSYOP Group
I Corps, DMZ

My name is Stanley Michelsen and I graduated from The United States Army Special Warfare School — Psychological Operations Enlisted Course on September 13, 1968. Before leaving Fort Bragg in March of 1969 I took part in around five or six James Gabriel Demonstrations. My station was the HB Combat PSYOP team broadcast section.

When I arrived in Vietnam in March of 1969, I was sent from 4th PSYOP Gp. Headquarters in Saigon to the 7th PSYOP Bn. in Da Nang. I was assigned to Company B and was soon on my way to Detachment 2 in Dong Ha with the 3rd Marine Division. My first team leader was Sgt. Ed Dulka (the Hulk). Hulk never liked being in the rear area so after each mission we'd take a day or two off before he'd move "his team" up the board to make sure that we would miraculously be the next team up in the rotation.

Hulk would teach me the ropes. We'd hit the chopper pad at Dong Ha Combat Base and fly in the CH-47 Chinook to Quang Tri Combat Base where we'd pick up our Kit Carson Scout and then off to the S-2 bunker at the Rock Pile. This is where we'd receive our intelligence briefing and broadcasting instructions (word for word what was to be said — nothing more). These instructions were very specific because Military Intelligence knew what NVA regiment was in the area and who they wanted to specifically target with our broadcasts.

These missions would take us to different Fire Support Bases – Neville, Russell, Dodge (Dodge was half-in and half-out of the DMZ at the 17th parallel in Quang Tri province). Other times we'd come in HOT to LZ's (landing zones) in and around the DMZ.

The last mission I did with Hulk (before I got my own team), we were with India 3/4 Marines on an LZ and being supported by Marine fire bases and Air Force jets with lots of Napalm bombs. The North Vietnamese Army had dissenting views about our being there and things were very tense. With a break in the action, a Marine sniper approached Hulk and asked for a word with him. They didn't move far away enough for me not to hear the conversation. The sniper was telling Hulk that it's no mistake that every time we broadcast, that very second, the NVA starts lobbing mortars into our position. He told us that we were killing Marines, and that if we broadcast again, we'd be dead men! I almost pissed my pants! What were we going to do? Hulk told him that he understood his point of view, but that if anything happened to us, another PSYOP team would soon be on the way to take our place. But the sniper's response was, "I'll deal with them when they get here. Right now…I'm only dealing with you." Then he turned and began walking away. Hulk looked at me shaking his head and asked if I'd heard any of that? I replied, "Fuck yeah, I heard that! What are we gonna do?" Hulk left for about 30 minutes. When he returned, he told me that a deal had been struck.

Long story short, seconds before our evening broadcast was to begin, a firefight broke out and our speakers were riddled with bullets. Things got quiet very fast and the NCOIC was quickly on us asking what happened. Hulk explained that some Marines witnessed NVA soldiers probing the wire and opened fire. The NCOIC asked who they were and they quickly came over and told their story. The story was accepted and we packed up our shit and were gone on the next chopper out.

When we finally got back to Dong Ha Combat Base and our hooch, we had a quick and very private meeting with the two other HB teams. We'd say nothing to any officers — number one. The other two teams had already suspected that at least some of our missions were to draw fire on purpose. And YES, Marines had been wounded and killed during these broadcasts. Would it have happened anyway? We were definitely as deep into their turf as one could get. Every second was spent in the "danger zone," but to this day, I know that the Marine sniper was on target.

We started bringing cases of beer with us on every mission, plus extra socks, noodles and canned ham. Whichever platoon the NCOIC would assign us to would always consider themselves lucky to have us. If we were humping through Tiger Tooth Mountain, we'd always help carry any of their extra ammo, mortar rounds or anything that would help the grunts out. Before we'd leave, they'd get all of our M-16 magazines and we'd take all of their bad ones (dented or springs gone bad) back with us to exchange. I'd leave my boots and socks and wear a ragged pair back to exchange for a new pair after every mission. Sometimes my pants and shirt would also be exchanged. Whatever they needed…I'd give it to them. We just put our PSYOP training to good use, but also our common decency for our fellow warriors.

Another thing I like to say is that I spent more time fighting as a Marine then I did doing PSYOP'S. I can't remember a single mission where I didn't expend every shell I had. PSYOPers deserve a Combat Badge. It's not just my humble opinion…it's a goddamn FACT!

Stanley Michelsen and Chad Spawr

John Harrison
Lieutenant, 3d Battalion 506th Parachute Infantry Regiment, 101st Airborne Division
Excerpt from John's book…
Steel Rain, the Tet Offensive 1968

"The Attack Of The Peacocks"

It was Lieutenant Len Liebler's first contact with the enemy, and we watched the whole thing unfold. Len's 3rd Platoon was moving in column formation across a draw when he made contact. The rest of Alpha Company was still up on top of the mountain that Len had just walked down from. We were in a climax forest up in the mountains near Cambodia. It was too high for jungle and the light underbrush of a climax forest made movement easy.

Second Platoon, my platoon, was acting as Alpha Company CP (Command Post) security and as a reaction force while the other three platoons of Alpha Company did clover-leaf patrols out from the mountain top where we had spent the previous night. Len's platoon, first out, had headed east, down the ridge and then through the draw until the shooting started.

When Len's point man saw movement in front of him, he had immediately fired a long burst, an entire magazine on full automatic from his M-16 into the brush in front of him. The slack man immediately faded right and followed suit with another long burst of fire. Meanwhile the rest of 3rd platoon had rapidly moved up on line to engage the enemy. It looked like textbook perfect Infantry battle drill in a combat situation.

Even from where I was on top of the mountain, about a football field and a half away, I could see flashes of what looked like bent over, dark forms, running low and fast through the brush; perhaps as many as 5 or 10 of them, darting quickly, back and forth, across the front of Len's platoon which was by then already all up on line, firing at them. Watching Len's platoon flow smoothly from a platoon column formation into a platoon on line was strangely attractive, almost elegant, if you like loud, violent, very dangerous, but nonetheless beautiful things.

I did not know it then, but it was really rare to actually see the enemy in a firefight. They were good at their job and the VC, like all good infantry, knew that what you can't see, you also can't shoot. Seeing them moving, even just in flashes through the brush should have told me something.

Then, I heard Len on the radio asking Captain Tom Gaffney for gunship support for an assault. Like me, Gaffney had come over to look when all the firing started and he too was standing near me on the military crest of the hill looking down on the draw. His RTO, (Radio Telephone Operator) was right beside him, just as mine was standing near me. We could all hear Len against a background of gunfire blaring loudly from the radios as he talked and also a little less loudly from the firefight a ways down the hill in front of us.

Gaffney and I watched as the action progressed below us. Since we were in a climax forest at the top of the mountains, rather than the jungle we had crawled through to get to the mountain's

110

base, we could see Len maneuver his platoon. Both of us were trying to figure out exactly what was going on. What had Len's platoon run into? I turned to my platoon and yelled, "Saddle up!" so that we would be ready to move if necessary.

When I looked back at Len's platoon in action, it appeared to me that there were even more bent over, dark forms running around in front of Len now. Had he found some of the famous black pajama clad, hard core, VC guerrillas?

I remember actually feeling a little twinge of jealousy that Len had gotten into them first. All the Alpha Company platoon leaders were very competitive, very aggressive. However, Tom Gaffney and I were way to far away to be sure what was going on below us in the draw. Neither of us carried the Army's almost useless but nonetheless heavy, 6x—power, field glasses. So we just stood there Tom and I, and stared.

In truth, we were both still trying to figure out what was going on below. What had Len gotten into? And then, I saw Gaffney begin to smile. So, I turned back to look where he was looking, but I did not see anything to smile about. However, Gaffney had lived in these mountains for months at a time on his last tour in Vietnam as a Green Beret, so he had experience that we did not yet have. This was Alpha Company's first search and destroy mission after our short orientation in country at Phan Rang. It was even our first set of clover-leaf patrols. Except for Gaffney and a few of others, we were all still green, very, very green.

Gaffney told Len "*No*" on the gunships and ordered him to advance immediately. A few minutes later, an obviously deflated Len called in to report that he had successfully attacked a flock of peacocks. Gaffney immediately corrected him and said:

"This is 6. A group of peacocks is called a cluster, and that is a good start for a word describing what just happened." Gaffney said evenly, but he was smiling broadly as he talked into

his radio handset…*"How many did you kill? Over…"* Gaffney asked.

"This is 3-6. A lot, over…" a now completely crestfallen Len replied.

"Good battle drill, 3–6. Finish your patrol. Alpha—6, out." Gaffney said, still smiling.

Tom turned, took a sip of coffee from his steaming canteen cup and walked back to the top of the hill, his RTO trailing behind him.

After hearing that, in spite of all the dead birds laying about I'll bet that Len was smiling too because Gaffney was very careful in giving praise. If he said the battle drill was good given his extensive combat experience as a Green Beret and earlier in the Korean War, there were few alive better able to judge it than Captain Tom Gaffney.

I found out later that a peacock can be over four feet long even without considering the length of the tail and it can weigh about fifteen pounds. They are really big, and more important they looked like even bigger birds. After s e e i n g t h e m r u n n i n g

through the brush from a distance, particularly the darker hens, I was glad that it was Len that had encountered them first. I would have attacked them too…no question. Of course, that did not stop us from harassing Len about it. Nothing could stop that. And, it had been good battle drill, not so good for the peacocks though.

Marty Hauser
FSB C2, DMZ
April 70 to January 71
Sp4 and Acting Jack (Sergeant)

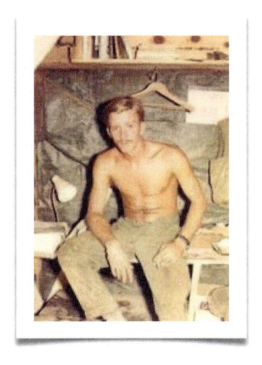

"Those packets all look the same!"

It was just another day on FSB C2, 1970, except that we were getting ready to go on an artillery raid. We were told that we were going into the A Shau, along the Laotian border, to support the 101st Airborne Division in Laos. When we finally got to our destination that afternoon, and after getting the guns set up, we proceeded to "dig in."

Being a mechanic, I had to dig my hole out by the guns. I began to dig and quickly realized that I was once again getting to experience that red clay that we all got to know so while well in

Vietnam. This time, however, the clay was dry instead of the muddy type that stuck to everything and made you feel like you had an added fifty pounds on your boots when you walked. So, the digging-in process was slow…after digging the rest of the day and into the night, I only had a hole about one foot deep. At this point, I told myself, "To hell with this." I found some of that half-round culvert that the engineers left lying around, covered the hole I had made, and began to sand bag it (I shouldn't really call them sand bags, since I had to fill them with chunks of hard clay which were more like rocks than sand!).

I was "beat to hell" when I finally finished, but I called the Lieutenant of B. Battery over for a cup of coffee. By this time of day and as tired as we both were, we were really looking forward to some coffee. I grabbed the C-rat box, got the coffee, got some C4, and made us each a cup. The Lieutenant asked for sugar, so I grabbed the sugar from the C-rat box, put it in his coffee and handed it to him. He was so anxious for that coffee that he took a large mouthful. But, before he could swallow it, it came spraying out of his mouth and all over me. He started to yell and me and asked me what the hell I done to his coffee…it was bitter as hell! I explained that I made it like I always do, but when I looked at the two empty sugar packets I had put into his coffee, I realized that it was salt, not sugar. I assumed I was really in "deep shit" at this point, but I guess he was just too tired to get made. Instead, we both had a good laugh over it and I made him another cup of coffee…he added the sugar to his!

So, if anyone knows who the Lieutenant who was with B. Battery around May 1970, please let me know. I'd like to buy him a cup of coffee and put the sugar in it for him this time. Maybe I can show him that I don't always "screw up" and that I turned out OK.

Dennis Smiser
1LT & Captain
6th PSYOP Battalion
Vietnam 1968-70

To say that my job in Vietnam was "unusual" would be an understatement. Although I was assigned to the 6th Psychological Operations Battalion, much of my time was spent in pursuit of non-traditional goals, one of which was identifying, locating, and taking "unwilling" enemy agents out of their hiding places and bringing them safely into protective custody.

Conducting these extraction operations was always difficult and dangerous and was usually completed in the presence of large concentrations of American infantry and armor. Typically, these extractions involved sealing the village with massive armed force and then entering the area to meet with the target of the extraction. This was always fraught with danger, as it would not have been unusual for the person to be armed and to trigger an ambush on the American officer coming for the actual extraction event.

One of these is especially memorable, as it involved one other member of the 6th PSYOP Battalion, who was accompanying a platoon from the 1st Cavalry Division. I knew when the seal operation would be completed, so I infiltrated the village the night before, met with the person I'd be extracting, and awaited the arrival of the armored-infantry force.

The person in question was a disgruntled North Vietnamese officer who desired to escape the war. Once the seal was in place, I escorted the man (known as a "Hoi Chanh") out into the village center so we'd be in full view of the American combat forces. I was fully armed with weapons and equipment, as I'd had to be prepared for any situation that might arise in this operation. This sudden appearance was a bit of a shock to many of the Americans, but the PSYOP team on the perimeter knew what was happening. I'm not sure they expected me to be there, but there we were.

We escorted my Hoi Chanh to a hasty landing pad, where an Army Huey had landed. We loaded aboard and quickly departed. I recall turning my new friend over to senior intelligence officers, and eventually returned to our battalion HQ for my next assignment.

Charles L. Hess
Chief Warrant Officer
US Army Counterintelligence
Military Assistance Command-Vietnam (MACV)
Vietnam 1970 - 1971

My Vietnam ventures began in September 1970 at Military Intelligence Battalion Headquarters in the coastal city of Nha Trang, where I would stay for a month while my undercover identification status as a Captain would be established at the Pentagon. I was a Warrant Officer WO-3 assigned to serve as an advisor to a battalion of 36 ARVN intelligence agents commanded by a Major, two Captains and one Lieutenant.

Although I was a Counterintelligence Warrant Officer in the US Army, I was reflagged as an Army Captain because the South Vietnamese Army had no respect whatsoever for any form of Warrant Officer. Making me a "temporary" Captain solved this problem. After a period of a few months, I became the "senior" Captain on our advisory team, which put me in position to do many things which I had no idea how to do.

When I left for Vietnam, I had to leave my family, consisting of my wife and two very young children, behind in St.

Louis, Missouri. My wife had located a place in Fenton, Missouri, which was actually our first house. We had a neighbor, who as it turns out was very old and senile, and who had no hesitation to say what was on his mind. One day while my young son Greg was out in the yard, this neighbor approached and asked why he had not seen me in quite a while. When Greg answered that I was in Vietnam, this neighbor told him that, "He would never see his Dad again."

As you can imagine, that shocked a very young boy and caused him great distress. My wife wrote me to tell me of this problem, and I immediately made arrangements to take my R&R leave and fly back to the US to help put my son's mind at ease.

While this may seem a relatively innocuous situation, the travel itself was problematic since I had to travel in military uniform and had no end of harassment and vile comments from my fellow passengers. It was not a pleasant trip. At one point, I had drifted off to sleep on the flight, and when I awoke, a nearby passenger was glaring angrily in my direction. His stare was direct and very unpleasant. I did not understand at the time why there was such hostility toward American servicemen, but I experienced it that day. I've never forgotten the way that immaculately dressed passenger glared at me.

The local MAC-V team would supply my logistical support, such as living quarters and meals. The only concern was if someone were to somehow learn of my true identity and blow the whole deal. That concern did not last very long, after all it was a war zone.

The ARVN Major and I quickly learned we were very compatible and immediately established a work routine. He spoke very limited English yet was intelligent and quick to acknowledge trends to our conversations. The Lieutenant (LT) had good use of English and was a welcome interpreter. He advised me not to stand when the Major entered my office because of my 6'2" height and the Major's 5'5" stature.

I learned to show respect in other ways. He began inviting me to join him for breakfast at his favorite restaurant not far from the compound and promised to never order something which maybe harmful. The meals usually consisted of a rice-based soup with various types of vegetables and occasional pieces of meat. One morning my curiosity got the best of me and I asked what the fatty substance was in the soup, which I had about half way down my throat. He said he did not know in English but made an oink sound and acknowledged the word pig then pointed to his head acknowledging the word brains. Thanks to the soup being very tasty, what was in my throat went where it was intended.

We also fell into a routine of visiting a restaurant across the street for a beer several times a week around 3 PM. It was a landmark in the town, very adorned with dragons and lions, and a popular meeting place for the locals. One afternoon we were detained by finishing a report on Viet Cong troop movements we wanted to submit to headquarters, when we were shaken out of our seats by the loudest of explosions. Sappers (assassins/insurgents) had blown up the landmark and killed four of our agents. I'm not saying the Major and I were targets, but the timing was right, and added more meaning to our battle cry, "They're everywhere".

The ARVN Major was promoted to Colonel and I was invited to the dinner, but not prepared. He requested two bottles of Cognac, which I got through the MAC-V hotel bar. On the afternoon of the celebration as I entered the compound in my beat-up jeep, slacks and short sleeve shirt, there was a long table with white table cloth, all set with South Vietnamese chinaware and utensils, and about 25 guests all dressed in their resplendent military and civilian dress, and they were each standing behind their chairs waiting for my arrival. No one had told me about the extent of the celebration, and I felt a bit conspicuous, but any tensions were eased as the Cognac was presented. My congratulations were offered at that time so there was no need for further "speeches."

The time to say, "Goodbye" finally came, but amazingly soon, and while the Colonel and I were exchanging well wishes, he held a short ceremony and presented me with the Dahn-Du Boi-Tinh Medal (Republic of Vietnam Armed Forces Honor) the highest award bestowed by South Vietnam during the war to any non-ARVN military member in a non-combat position, such as advisor or cadre trainer. It is an honor I do not wish to forget.

This ties in with another incident in which I had made friends with a young American Major assigned to the MAC-V team. He was married with a wife and two young children, and was my age. One afternoon we were walking in town with our counterparts just for relaxation, when a sapper stepped out of a doorway and shot off the top of his head killing him instantly and then ran through the street with no one trying to stop him. Had I been leading the foursome...? They were everywhere! Not confined to rice paddies, banana plantations, jungles, foxholes, everywhere!

The American Emergency Ordnance Demolition (EOD) Team was active in our province, and our agents were eager to assist them by reporting caches of ordnance left behind by allied forces departing the area. I assisted the EOD on numerous occasions and was visiting their home base at Cam Rahn Bay the night sappers infiltrated the perimeter and detonated the ammo supply dumps about one quarter mile away. It was a fireworks display I never want to witness again.

Another incident occurred one evening when returning to the MAC-V hotel. There was a note from the CIA asking for my presence at their hotel about two blocks away at 7 pm. We had met several times at intelligence briefings and I felt a sense of obligation, which was shattered when all they wanted was a sixth person for a game of charades. My mind was incensed and I let it be known. I never again subjected myself to their nonsense and the dangers of walking the streets alone at dusk in a highly dangerous area.

Eventually my DEROS time arrived and I had to report to our Battalion Headquarters in Nha Trang. The Commanding Officer, a Colonel, had been sent home for alcoholism and the First Sergeant was Acting Commander. As I walked onto the compound, my welcoming committee was a dirty little mutt wearing a Bronze Star as a collar. I saw absolutely no humor in it and when it was awarded to me the next day, I declined it and accepted my fifth Meritorious Service Medal. My mind was scrambled and not thinking properly, and I still regret that decision fifty-three years later.

Thomas Sweeney
Specialist 5
HHC 4th Psychological Operations Battalion
Saigon, Vietnam

Being assigned to a Psychological Operations (PSYOP) unit did not always mean going into the field to drop leaflets or playing loudspeaker messages. Those leaflets being thrown from a low-flying aircraft had to be printed by someone.

I was one of the printers who produced the leaflets in the millions. I held the rank of US Army Specialist 5, military occupational specialty code (MOS) 23F2W (Offset Pressman). I had graduated from the New York City School of Printing in 1965 and worked in the printing trade from 1965 to 1967 before being drafted into the Army in July 1967.

After Basic Combat Training, I was assigned to the John F. Kennedy School for Special Warfare at Ft. Bragg, NC, for a seven-week course on Psychological Operations prior to deployment to Vietnam. I arrived in Vietnam on December 12, 1967, and was assigned to print leaflets for the 4th PSYOP Group. The printing section was located on the righthand side of the Cruz Compound, the Group's assigned area in Saigon. It consisted of one van with a paper cutter, two vans, each with two 2-color offset web printing presses

capable of printing one color on each side of the paper or two colors in line; and one van for making negatives and plates for printing. The paper weight was 16 or 20-pounds. One of the 2-color printers would run any weight paper, but the other would only print 20 pound paper. If you put 16-pound paper on it, the web would break, and the paper would wrap around the blanket cylinder. You had to play close attention to what you were doing.

The vans had ramps on which rolls of paper could be brought from the motor pool on skids and unloaded, then rolled to the back doors of the 2-color offset printing press capable ot running one color on the back side and 2-colors on the front side of the sheet. There was also a single color sheet-fed multi-lith offset printing press which was used to print newsletters.

123

When printing was completed, the roll paper was cut down to sheets of 8.5" x 11" on the press and forwarded to the "delivery." A word of explanation here: the back of the press is called the "feed" (where the roll of paper is loaded) and the "delivery" is where  the paper comes out at the front of the press.

The Battalions (individual units of the 4th Group) had a special tool they called a "fork" that was used to remove the paper when the delivery pile reached about two feet in height. The "fork" was needed because it could remove the paper without turning off the press. Nothing stopped the press in the middle of a run. The paper was then brought outside to be cut down to leaflet-size by civilian Vietnamese employees. We worked twelve hour shifts, seven days a week unless we had guard duty. If a pressman was on guard duty, then someone else had to be assigned to that press so that it never stopped running.

The offset plates that were used would wear out way early due to improper foundation solution. The basic theory of offset printing is that grease and water don't mix. The ink, which is the greasy part, and the fountain solution which is water and Gum Arabic mixed together to a proper percentage of hydrogen, better known as "PH." The fountain solution wets the plate. When the ink comes in contact only the sensitized areas will accept the ink. There were times we didn't have any of the solution and ran on plain tap water. The acidity level of the water ate up the plates. Eventually, they sent the plate-maker to Japan to learn how to make bio-metal plates. When the image began to wear out on those plates, we would apply sulphuric acid to the plate and the

124

image would reappear. Those plates were supposed to be good for million printing impressions.

The paper cutter was old and needed repairs. The cutting was done by civilian Vietnamese employees cutting the 8.5"x11" sheets down to size the safety switch "off." They were constantly told to leave the safety on because it would sometimes double-cut the sheets. I was working on the 3-color offset press in the hut one day when a Vietnamese employee ran in screaming. He lifted up his arm and blood came squirting out; the cutter had double-cut when he was removing the paper and took his hand off. I grabbed him and prepared a tourniquet by wrapping my belt around his arm to stop the bleeding. Some men from the office took him to the local hospital. I went straight to the cutter and secured his hand in the hope they could put it back on his arm. Three months later he returned with no hand. His name went form "Papa-san" to "Stumpy."

Near the end of my tour in late 1968 the two web presses in the vans were being removed and placed in a room in the back of the Cruz Compound where the motor pool and generators were. I don't know if that move was ever completed.

I left Vietnam on December 12, 1968, and a couple of the guys sent me Christmas cards which I still have. I returned to the printing trade in July 1969. I apprenticed as a Printing Press Operator until 1974. I was promoted to Journeyman Press Operator and worked in the trade until 1984, when I was hired by the New York City Police Department as a Printing Press Operator. Over the years, I moved up from the Bindery Foreman to Deputy Director of Printing, then to Director of Printing Services. I ran the entire Printing services for the NYPD with 30 personnel assigned to my command. I retired on July1, 2009 after 25 years of service to the New York Police Department.

Kerry Cooper
198th Light Infantry Brigade
23d (Americal) Division
May 70 – May 71

First week of May 1971, I was up again for promotion to E5. Waiting for orders to go back to company Head Quarters I'm sitting in the dark waiting to see who's going out on ambush. The Platoon Sergeant comes up and tells me I'm heading in but on an Emergency Leave. Neither he nor the Lieutenant know why. It was an even more uncomfortable night that night, wondering what happened…was it my dad, one of my sisters or brothers, no idea if one of them is sick, hurt or maybe dead?

Next morning we moved out at first light and picked up the night ambush patrol. The next week is much the same routine. Walk awhile, split off on patrols and meet up down the trail. Eventually we link up with the rest of the company. World comes that resupply, C-Rats and other resupply is on the way. And then my platoon sergeant says get your shit ready Coop your going in.

Three days later, orders in hand, I'm driven to a chopper that takes me to Chu Lai, then after check in I board a flight to Saigon. Then rushed to a commercial flight to Japan. There, it's a 3 hour layover.

Fly then to San Francisco, same plane to Ft.Worth/Dallas International. Plane lands at Ft.Worth end of airport. Then practically running to get to the Dallas end of the airport I barely make it to my connecting flight. Damn! Its the same plane & crew?

Then I'm off on a non-stop flight to Birmingham Alabama, that takes me to Atlanta for a connecting flight back to Birmingham. Anxious to get home to finally get to find out why I was sent home, I find out my brother Wally is in jail for shooting my oldest sister's boyfriend. Nobody's dead or in the hospital and my dad is out with his girlfriend. By the way, he was 81 and she was 78 back then. How they got me home is a mystery. I stayed long enough to see Wally at the jail, see the author of my Dear John letter & husband, a few friends and then arrange to go back to Vietnam. And by the time I got back to Company HQ, someone else got my promotion. And that wasn't the end of my May. I found out that my cousin Jeffery Cooper was KIA the day after I left to go home.

127

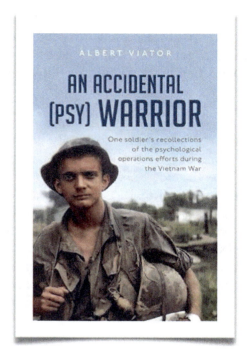

"Give Me Your Hand"

I have thought of Private Washington often whenever race issues have come to the attention of us all. Much more so in recent years with the Black Lives Matter movement and the systemic unjust race and policing issues that have been so much in the news.

With all the popularity of virtual gaming devices I've thought it would be great if the technology could be used to place race haters into virtual combat situations like many of the real-life situations I've discussed in this book. Let the hater see how it feels to have his life dependent on the Black guy next to him laying out in the rain on a night ambush or fording a river, up to his neck in the rushing current while carrying 40 pounds of gear trying to keep his footing when he hears the booming voice of a guy like Private Washington call out, "Give me your hand."

Private Washington was tall, strong, and Black. He could see that I was barely making progress fighting the heavy current as our infantry patrol forded a fast-moving river during the rainy season in the pineapple plantations southeast of Saigon.

Each step I took had been a struggle and I'd slipped under the surface more than once as the river bottom suddenly fell away. When I finally did get next to the river's edge the hard, slippery, mud banking made it impossible for me to get my footing and climb out. I was exhausted, leaning against the banking catching my breath when I heard the deep baritone voice over my head, "Give me your hand." I passed him my gear and held my arms up over my head as he reached and plucked me out of the water with one hand like you'd pick up a little kid playing in the yard. I remember my boots being pulled free of the sucking mud at the riverbank and being lifted up onto the shore like a little kid.

I thanked him as I was gathering up my gear, telling him how much I appreciated his help. He replied simply, "Yah, I could see you were fighting the current."

No big deal, he was just helping a fellow soldier who needed a hand. That's how it went between all us guys during my tour of Nam.

I know there was considerable racial unrest between black and white soldiers in some parts of Vietnam, mostly in the Central and Northern part of the country and particularly in the later years of the war. I'm not going to make any value judgments one way or the other, "Just saying," as in the vernacular of today.

But in III Corp, when I was attached to the 25th or the 1st Infantry Divisions, or throughout my time with the 199th Light Infantry Brigade, I never witnessed or was affected by, or even heard about any race issue among the soldiers with whom I served. If anything, the predominant vibe was that we were all in this together and related to and depended on each other equally.

Marty Hauser
FSB DZ
April 1970 - Jan. 1971
SP-4 and Acting Jack

Orienting The New "Boot" To Incoming

Well, it was one of those rare days when my buddy, Dan, and I got to go to Dong Ha for the day. You know how that goes… once the guys know you're doing to the rear, they start giving you their orders for things they need from the PX, laundry to be taken or picked up, film to be taken for developing, etc. While we were waiting for the morning mine sweep to clear the road to Cam Lo, we took everyone's orders. Once we got to Dong Ha, we did our thing, but before leaving, we always checked at the transit hooch for new boots going back to the Battery.

This particular day, we had a new boot for maintenance. He got his gear, got into the back of the 3/4s ton and we headed back to C2. If you remember, when you got in country, no one talked to you much or explained what to expect out there on the

FSB. It was no different this time. We didn't explain anything to "Red" (we named him that because he had red hair).

Upon arriving at C2, I took Red over to Top's bunker for the "new boots speech." It was around 4:00 pm when Top finished his little speech (back then 4:00 pm was the typical time of day for incoming). Just as I was taking Red back to the maintenance bunker, it started.

On the first round, we hit the dirt. Then I jumped up and ran for the nearest bunker. I assumed Red was behind me, but when I got to the bunker and turned around, he wasn't there. I thought to myself, SHIT, where the hell did this go? I had to find him, so I started going from bunker to bunker to look for him but had no luck. Then it occurred to me that the only place I hadn't looked was the gun pits.

I started checking the pits and sure enough that's where I found him hiding. We managed to get back to the maintenance bunker and when things settled down, I had a nice long talk with him. I explained to him where to hide and where not to hide when incoming is happening.

From that day on, I made a point of talking to the "new boots" in maintenance and explaining what to do when we got incoming. I sure wish someone had done that for me.

Rod Fritz
Specialist 4
4th Psychological Operations Group
11th Armored Cavalry Regiment
Vietnam 1969-1970

My name is Rod Fritz and I joined the United States Army in June of 1968, shortly after graduation from college in New England. I joined because the draft was hot and heavy at the time and the Vietnam War was the place most draftees ended up. I did not want to be that draftee. I was told upon my signing up that I could attend any A-I-T I wanted, and I wanted Journalism at Ft. Benjamin Harrison, Indiana.

After Basic training in Ft. Jackson, I was sent to Indiana at the Defense Information School (DINFOS). I succeeded in Journalism class and continued on at DINFOS for Broadcast Specialist School. After graduation my orders came for Ft. Gordon, Georgia and I ended up working in the video and training film section of the Signal Corps. A short while later, my orders came for Vietnam. I was not worried; I am a Broadcast Specialist a

71R20. I will end up at Armed Forces Radio and Television, AFVN, or so I thought.

After a 30-day leave, I reported to Ft. Dix, New Jersey for my flight to Vietnam. I arrived in Vietnam July 5, 1969. After a short hop to Long Binh, I got my orders for the 4th PO Group in Saigon. What? I have no MOS for the Post Office and questioned a Sergeant at Long Binh regarding the 4th PO Group. I was told it isn't the Post Office it's Psychological Operations. What the hell? Never heard of it in my short time in the Army and figured there must be some mistake. I belong on Armed Forces Radio.

After reporting to Group headquarters in Saigon, I told the First Sergeant that I was a Broadcast Specialist and there must be some mistake on my orders. "Not at all," said First Sargent, "the 71R20 MOS is assigned to PSYOPS because you have been trained to operate a tape recorder." Made no sense to me, but then, this is the Army PFC Fritz. I was assigned to the 6th PSYOP Battalion in Bien Hoa and ended up being a "flyer" working with the 5th Special Operations Squadron of the Air Force. I flew most days my first five months of my tour, dropping leaflets and playing propaganda tapes over loudspeakers from the fixed wing aircraft. I flew in C-47's, U-10's and O-2's. In early January I was ordered to the "field" and assigned to the 11th Armored Cavalry Regiment based at Quan Loi. Lots of **"red dirt"** in Quan Loi!!!!!

Shortly after my arrival in Quan Loi, I was informed there was a pirate radio station operated by the 11th ACR. I immediately contacted those running the station and in a few short days, after they found out about my DJ background, I was ON THE AIR. I worked Psychological Operations during the day, flying in Huey's or Loach choppers or heading out in a convoy to local villages to win the "hearts and minds" of the locals. During the evening, I was "Lucky" Fritz on WACR Radio Blackhorse. I did Oldies shows, Folk shows, Soul shows and even some special radio shows

134

and always taking requests. It was a terrific job to have, even if it wasn't my assigned job. I still have tapes of some of my shows from WACR and if you would like to hear one, Check out this website online: AFRTS Archive: WACR Radio Blackhorse, Vietnam 1970.

All in all, a good time at WACR, the studio was on top of the Officer's Mess and the equipment was darn good. I have no idea how these radio turntables, tape recorders and more ever got to Quan Loi, and I didn't ask. I stayed in Quan Loi with the 11th ACR until middle of June 1970 when I returned to Bien Hoa to get ready to return home. Of note here, I also participated in the Cambodia invasion in May 1970. Some scary stuff to say the least. But I always had WACR to return to at the end of missions during the day.

Once, while on R & R in Australia, the radio station took a hit from mortars fired by "Charlie" and the person filling in on my show was hit with some shrapnel. To be clear, he was not wounded badly. When I returned to Quan Loi after R & R, the guys all said the VC and NVA were upset that I wasn't on the air. And that's why the station was hit. I will say that after returning to the air broadcasting my shows, there were no more attacks near the studio. Go figure!!!

I have included here a picture of my early arrival in Vietnam, flying a U-10 fixed-wing aircraft, as well as a picture of me at the Quan Loi WACR station. Quan Loi, compared to Bien Hoa, was no picnic…lots of red clay, and "Charlie" was always around to let us know he was there.

I made it home after Vietnam, serving my remaining time in the Army at the Public Information Office (PIO) at Ft. Jackson, South Carolina. I left the Army in June of 1971 and began a long career in Radio and Television. I worked on the air in Easton, PA, Philadelphia, Denver, Tampa-St Pete and over 40 years in Boston.

Welcome Home to all my Brothers and Sisters who served, not only in Vietnam, but around the work.

Rod "Lucky" Fritz

Radio Blackhorse

I've included a picture of a U-10 Courier, one of the small planes in which we flew PSYOP missions. We called it the "Vomit Comet" because the pilots pretended they were fighter jocks and contorted us all over the sky, especially when we were flying missions over enemy territory, ongoing battles, etc. We literally had to lean backward over the seat and hand-throw the leaflets out a small chute. If it was a loudspeaker flight, we had to lean backward to load the tape cassettes into the broadcast equipment. More than one lunch or dinner went out that little leaflet chute!

Raymond Ambrozak
Captain, Infantry
US Army
6th Psychological Operations Battalion
4th Psychological Operations Group
Military Assistance Command Vietnam (MACV)
1964-65, 1966-67, 1970-71

Ann and I had talked about one day going on vacation to Hawaii. Being deployed to an active war zone, at the time of the vacation, was not part of the plan. We were a little young to be thinking about a bucket list, but my chosen profession put a different perspective on many things.

One of the items you would find in every soldier's billet throughout Vietnam was a calendar. The war had made certain dates days to remember on the countdown to be homeward bound. The final date was usually circled and had a lot of artwork to show its significance. The first date that was the subject of a countdown, was the first day the R&R would begin for that soldier. It was the first day for the world to begin to make sense again. It was the day that seeing his family would not be just a dream. Not only was the R&R providing a prayerful relief from the thankless task of bringing the two Vietnams together, but the R&R was in Hawaii!!!

Hawaii kept its part of the bargain as an idyllic tropical paradise. Our first night in Honolulu was interrupted by a spasm that hit me about 3 AM, causing a flash fever that put me in a sweat. It didn't last long, but it put me first in line at the ER for a very thorough exam which did not result in anything other than an appointment for the following day. I was pleased that whatever it was, did not put me in the hospital, because I had a secondary mission to accomplish. The mission was to find and purchase a needed gear for a motion picture projector which had been given to our team by an Air Force unit when they departed our area. It was our only source of entertainment and was limping along through continuous breakdowns. Rubber bands, glue, and screws in the wrong holes were the only things keeping it going. It was in the third camera shop, that we found the gear which the shopkeeper did not want to sell as it was on his demo unit. After an explanation of what life was like in the central highlands of Vietnam, he ended up giving us the demo model. The daily visits to the lab did not reveal anything that could not be diagnosed by shower shoes Wilson, longtime icon of Vietnam, who said, "You caught somethin' that is not too bad."

We squeezed in as much dining and dancing as we could each day. I was much better at dining than dancing, but Ann made us look good on the dance floor. The only thing bothering me was my watch. As I saw the hands move, my mind wondered if those routine things were being done at the time they were supposed to. The hands of that watch would also take me back to my final 180 days.

On the walk back to our hotel, we decided to have a night cap. Looking around the block we were in, there were several to choose from. Shipwreck Kelly's looked like a good choice. As we entered, we heard the music — not too loud — songs we knew — perfect. After several songs, the band leader did as many were doing in those days, asked if there anyone here from Vietnam? I got a picture in my mind of the demonstrators in the news I had seen recently before I raised my hand. A few heads turned my way when the band leader asked if I had a request.

Things got a little quieter as I rose to my feet. In a loud clear voice (I had to make this good) I said, "The Baltimore Colts Fight Song." The band leader talked to 2 or 3 band members. They stood and began a lively version of the song. Some of the crowd joined in for 3 stanzas. We gave a tip of the hat to the band leader and called it a day. It had been a good one. You couldn't ask for better than that.

The following day was our last goodbye. Hawaii delivered one of her picture postcard days. We agreed earlier to a night cap at Shipwreck Kelley's to top off a great R&R. As we entered the room, the band was going full bore. When the band leader saw us, he brought the band to a full stop, then broke into The Baltimore Colts Fight Song. Perfect end to a perfect day.

The mysterious illness turned out to be malaria, which gave me a ride home on a med-evac flight after eleven months in-country.

Author Note: *In 1971, while serving as Senior District Advisor in Phu Nhon District in Pleiku Province, Ray was awarded the Silver Star for heroism in a major firefight with enemy forces between 15-16 March. Ray had been "trained" for the role of Senior District Advisor, a role he assumed in 1971. Here is the background to his last Vietnam assignment:*

The District Senior Advisor Program (DSA) was the brainchild of someone in the State Department's Foreign Service Institute. Its purpose was to select personnel to be trained as advisors to specific District Chiefs in VN. The POI (Program of Instruction} looks as if it was created by a PsyOperator.

One of the key features was that the DSA. was provided with current information about the district he was to be assigned upon entering country. When I arrived and began processing, it was for an assignment to a district other than the one to which I was trained at the Foreign Service Institute. My raising hell about the screwing up the beginning of my third tour, seemed to only spur them on until a message marked urgent was shown, saying "the next school trained DSA to step off a flight arrival was to have his orders changed.

It was later that afternoon that the DPA collared me and we went to his BOQ for a briefing. His description of the district took a full hour before the officer, a Lieutenant Colonel (LTC) took a breath, at which time he poured two fingers of J. W. (Johnnie Walker) and slammed them down. My first words were, "LTC, you gotta be shi--ing me!"

"I wish I were," was his stone-faced reply.

"How much overlap with the present DSA will I have?" I replied.

"None — he can't help you. He gets off the chopper and you get on. You will have 3 days of briefings."

No one ever accused this LTC of sugar-coating any operation for which he was responsible.

Hammond Salley

Major (Retired)
US Army Infantry

"Needs of The Service"

Temporary Army assignments based on "needs of the service" can open the door to many unexpected and unusual experiences. Similarly, the term "Other Duties as Assigned" has found many young Lieutenants on duty rosters for "Officer of The Guard" "Officer of The Day" "Courtesy Patrol Officer" "Mess Officer" or "Slot Machine Inventory Officer" etc.

Such temporary extra duties are fairly standard and one learns to adapt. However, during my military career, I chanced to wind up on several out of the ordinary and very unusual assignments — at least for me. I'll mention a few and conclude with one during my second tour in Vietnam.

The Small Arms Test Committee:

I had just returned from my first tour in Vietnam to attend the year long "Advanced Officer's Course" at The Infantry School, Ft. Benning, GA. However, as it turned out, the course I was to attend wouldn't start for several more months. Accordingly, to fill the time, early arriving officers were given temporary assignments until classes started. I wound up at The Small Arms Test Committee. These were the folks that tested all new small arms for possible adoption or rejection by the Army. Although I never tested any weapons, I was given small chores and observed and learned a lot from the experts. I was fascinated by one of the test weapons — the Special Purpose Individual Weapon (SPIW) — which fired a flechette: a small pointed, fin-stabilized, steel projectile. It was never adopted though.

Ranger School Experiment:

I was fortunate to be assigned to ROTC duty between Vietnam tours. My family and I really enjoyed the academic atmosphere. However, my summers were spent as Cadre at ROTC summer camps at distant military posts. I spent six weeks at Ft. Riley, KS my first summer and was expecting to do the same the second year. Then I was notified that the Army was going to experiment with sending ROTC juniors to nine weeks of Ranger School instead of the normal ROTC summer camp. That way, all graduating Ranger Students would be wearing the Ranger Tab as ROTC seniors at their respective colleges. One Ranger qualified officer from each Army ROTC area was assigned as a Tactical officer to monitor and grade one platoon of Ranger students through the training. I was selected to represent the 5th Army area and found myself going through Ranger School a second time. The program was a success and helped me get in better shape. After some reflection, I decided that this was the best training for my return to Vietnam the following month.

The CG-4A Glider Incident:

I had completed my tour as an Airborne Battalion S-3 in the 82nd Airborne Division and wound up as the Deputy G-5 for Civil-Military Operations in the Division Headquarters. Someone thinking I must have had nothing better to do, I was assigned to also monitor the 82nd Airborne Division Museum. The Museum is actually a wonder of the Division's history from Sgt. York and on to WW-II, etc. In many respects, this additional duty was an honor.

One day I was called in to see the Division Commander. He asked me what the museum was missing in the way of the Division's history. Of course, I had no idea what the right answer was — so he told me. "There is no WW-II glider on display at the museum. Get one." I said, "Roger Out" and left to find a WW-II glider without the slightest idea about where to start looking. Someone recommended trying the Air Force Museum at Wright-Patterson AFB in Dayton, OH. I managed to contact the curator of the museum who was very helpful in saying that he would check his sources. I received a call from him a month later indicating that he had found one on a farm in northern Ohio and that the farmer wanted $100 for the glider. I flew to Dayton, linked up with the curator and we drove to meet the farmer. He walked us out to the back 40 acres and, lo and behold, there was a CG-4A glider lying on the ground next to a barbed wire fence with the wings leaning up against the fence. The covering canvas was in taters and the instruments were all there but the glass was broken. Being a skeptical novice in restoration, the curator assured me that the glider was, in fact, a jewel of a find. I asked the farmer how it got on his field and he told me that it was already there when he purchased the farm years ago — and therefore had no idea.

I paid the farmer the $100, arranged for a local National Guard truck to pick it up and bring it to Wright-Patterson. I had also arranged for a Massachusetts Guard C-130 to fly it to Pope

AFB where I pick it up and took it to the museum. Before I left for my next PCS assignment, the curator called and told me why he believed the glider was in the farm field. Apparently, at the end of WW-II, there were tons of military surplus items on sale, and crated gliders were sold for $15. Farmers were buying them, discarding the gliders and using the upright crates as outhouses. Apparently Sears and Roebuck sold their outhouses for $30.

I was given another mission to obtain a C-119 Flying Boxcar. I had similar frustrations in trying to locate one but finally managed to obtain a C-119 from the West Virginia Air Guard – the last flying Squadron in the United States. It was flown to Pope Air Force Base where I signed for a perfect flyable aircraft and proceeded to take the wings off so we could tow it through miles of telephone wires and street lights to the museum. It was reassembled wherein it still sits on it's concrete pad.

Carnival Meister:

I received orders assigning me to the 1st Battalion, 15th Infantry in Kitzingen, Germany. When I arrived, I found that my potential job as Executive Officer of the Battalion was still filled and I would be assigned to the Community Headquarters in the interim. Then I found that it was German/American Friendship Week and Carnival time and I was further assigned as the Community Carnival Meister to oversee setup and operations. Again, another assignment without any prior knowledge about carnivals — in this case, a real German carnival on base with the usual carnival rides and booths. There were also military vehicle displays, dunking booths, beer tent, etc. The attraction for soldiers and dependents were the rides. The major attraction for the German visitors, and there were lots of them, was the American Ice Cream. Apparently the normal German ice cream was just "Eis" or German Gelato. American ice cream is rich and creamy and was not available in German stores at the time. Anyway, we set up a booth and freezer trailer full of commissary ice cream. With German Customs present, we sold over $150,000 worth of ice cream to the local German visitors.

Freedom Hill Recreation Center:

During my second tour in Vietnam, I was assigned as the Deputy G-5 for Psychological Operations, 24th Corps Headquarters in Da Nang. As the Vietnam War was winding down for American combat troops, their missions were being acquired by South Vietnamese units. Accordingly, 24th Corps was deemed excessive and replaced by a more downsized organization: First Regional Assistance Command or FRAC. Out of the blue, I was asked if I wanted to take command of a local installation until it was also stood down. As I had previously worked as the XO of a Military Community in Germany, I indicated that I was interested. This installation was the Freedom Hill Recreation Center, famous for the number of celebrities who, over many years, had put on USO shows there for the troops. The installation included a big PX, bowling alley, movie theater, cafeteria, USO and Red Cross facilities, and, of course, a big outdoor amphitheater for the USO shows. We hosted the last USO show in Da Nang with Sammy Davis, Jr, performing.

Never, in my wildest imagination, had I ever visualized this type of duty — especially in Vietnam. There were hundreds of Vietnamese employees on the compound every day. As we were on the periphery of Da Nang, security was my major concern. Although Vietnamese units were in place, only one American brigade stood between us and the DMZ. Most of my troops comprised the day/night security elements. Both entry and departure were through gate security checks and the compound was emptied every evening. I managed to "secure" some additional weapons and bulldozed the entire perimeter of the compound for better observation.

Then it came time to turn over the compound to the Vietnamese Army. Lots of work was involved as all the various facilities had to be vacated: theater seats and projectors removed and shipped, big facility air conditioners removed, PX, USO and Red Cross emptied, etc. The biggest project was to remove the 20 lane bowling alley. A specialist from Brunswick arrived with a power saw and two large trucks. We dismantled the pin setting machines and loaded them on the truck. Then he cut each lane into three sections which we then hand carried onto the second truck. Apparently, the whole alley was being shipped to another location in the Pacific area for reconstruction.

Anyway, we met the imposed deadline for turning the facility over to the Vietnamese. The April Offensive commenced shortly thereafter.

Chad Spawr
1st Brigade 1st Infantry Division
MACV Advisory Team 47
6th Psychological Operations Battalion
1st Cavalry Division (Airmobile)
Vietnam 1967 – 1969

"A Dog Named Bear"

In November 1967, I was assigned to the 1st Brigade of the Big Red One, the famed 1st Infantry Division, then located near the town of Phuoc Vinh. Our team consisted of a 1st Lieutenant, a Staff Sergeant, three Spec 4's, and a PFC. We also had a South Vietnamese Sergeant assigned to us an interpreter. That seemed a bit superfluous, as our Staff Sergeant and I had been trained in the Hanoi dialect of the Vietnamese language. However, native language skills are always superior to recently trained barely articulate American enlisted soldiers.

In addition to our fellow team members, we had acquired our own mascot, a yellow male dog who appeared to be part golden Labrador. His name was Bear. He weighed about 40 pounds and stood about knee-high to those of us on the team. I don't think we ever knew how old Bear was, but he was very friendly, good-natured, loved to play catch with anything we'd throw for him to retrieve. Bear hated rats significantly!

Shortly after arriving at Phuoc Vinh, our Brigade relocated north to a rubber plantation called Quan Loi. The camp was built around a laterite dirt runway that was capable of handling recon, observation and C130 cargo aircraft, and which was also home to a large number of American Huey UH-1 helicopters. When we'd occasionally go for an exercise run up and down the runway, Bear would always join us, keeping pace with us, often dodging between our legs as we ran.

Bear slept in the hooches that were constructed for our troops, always sleeping near one of our bunks. He was usually a good house guest, although when he was sound asleep and fully relaxed, he emitted clouds of noxious gas that could rust the metal on our weapons. No matter! Bear was our team mascot, and who doesn't fart when needed?

Our team Staff Sergeant had a good friend who was a Senior Sergeant in the Scout Dog platoon at Quan Loi, and he was able to "negotiate" real dog food for Bear. The price was often some form of souvenir taken from the field, but we were usually able to give Bear a good food supply. On occasion, we supplemented his diet with GI food that we didn't want, but he loved it.

When our team was moved to An Loc and became an element of the MACV Advisory Team, Bear went with us. It was unusual that he left the basecamp, but he rode in our truck the few miles to An Loc, and barked at anything along the nasty laterite road that he thought merited attention. Upon arrival, we unloaded the truck, moved into our 4-man hootch and set up our accommodations. Bear moved in with us. It just seemed completely natural.

Our MACV compound had been a part of an old French facility. As in so many other cases in a combat zone, housing areas were often infiltrated by rats. These were large, aggressive and nasty rats. They weren't even shy about their presence...it was as if they objected to our very presence, and constantly plagued our hootch, crapped and pissed all over the place, and did not hesitate to move freely about our hootch. Being a small and confined space, we were not free to open fire with our weapons on them.

Early in our stay, Bear decided that he would solve our rat problem, and he promptly began taking them out one at a time. He would kill them and then take their bodies out by the main gate and leave them. After a few weeks, our rat population was dramatically reduced; even the size of the rats he killed had declined as it seemed he'd found several rat nests and killed their offspring. He never ate them.

Bear was our buddy, he loved to play, but he never left the compound when we went out on operations. We would not put him at risk going into potential combat operations, and he could not be used as a scout dog or other kind of dog used by the Army. When we left, he'd sit at the gate watching us go; when we returned he was waiting, barking, tail wagging and happy as we re-entered the compound. He was such a great morale asset for our team.

I was transferred from An Loc back to Long Binh in June 1968. I didn't see Bear again until early 1969 when I was leading PSYOP missions for the 1st Cavalry Division. We were traveling through An Loc, and I detoured to the old MACV compound. I stood at the main gate and hollered for Bear. Within seconds, he appeared from behind a building, ran to the gate, and barked at me.

His tail was beating the air as I entered the compound and roughed him up a bit as we'd done earlier. I sat on the ground with him briefly, but then he got distracted by some other dogs, and ran off to play. I never saw Bear again after that.

Epilogue

"I came home from Vietnam over fifty years ago...
Sometimes I'm still there." (Anonymous)

For many of us who served in Vietnam, the war didn't simply end when we came home. For most veterans, coming home was the end of one chapter in our lives, and the beginning of "the rest" of our lives. For so many, the "rest of our lives" would have a flavor few non-veterans could ever understand.

There were many ways that Vietnam stayed with us in our post-war lives. For so many veterans, the scourge of PTSD, complications from Agent Orange exposure, life-altering medical conditions, and the disabilities caused by serious wounds have affected our lives every living day.

In addition to these, there were often other "less well known" issues that have arisen. As an example, I returned to duty at Ft. Bragg, NC, in July 1969, where I was assigned to the 1st PSYOP Battalion. It was generally quiet and routine duty. I had begun noticing a distinct disorientation and a dizziness as I stood up after sitting for an extended period. It became progressively worse over a period of weeks. One morning, I went on "sick call" to see what was happening.

The doctor, an Army Green Beret captain, began a full physical examination. He stopped when he began looking in my ears. I recall him saying, "I think we've found the problem." He put some kind of instrument in my ear canal and began moving it back and forth and in slow circles. It was mildly uncomfortable, but bearable. After a few minutes, he extracted a thick greasy plug of dark red ear wax. It had plugged my ear canal completely. He asked me "Were you in Vietnam?" The answer was obvious.

He then performed the same procedure on my other ear, extracting another plug of dark red wax. I suddenly felt much better, less prone to slight dizziness. My hearing seemed to improve as well. Dr. Jeffrey McDonald, the Green Beret doctor, had found the source of my problem, resolved it, and made a big difference in my life at that moment. (As a footnote, Dr. McDonald was later found guilty in 1979 for the murder of his pregnant wife and two daughters at Ft. Bragg in 1970. It was a real blow to the US Army in general, as well as for the Special Forces community in particular.)

While I remember that incident, I also fully appreciate the fact that he solved my problem of dizziness and balance by cleaning that greasy dark red Vietnam dirt from my ears. Vietnam had indeed followed me home.

The numbers speak for themselves. Of the 2.7 million Americans who served in Vietnam, 58,479 were killed "In Country," over 300,000 were wounded by enemy action; since coming home, 22 veterans are committing suicide every single day. In total, after more than fifty years since the end of the war, over 1,000,000 Vietnam veterans have died from all causes since coming home.

One of the major post-war effects has been the widening effects of the use of Agent Orange, a defoliant sprayed widely by the US to take away the heavy jungle or forested areas under which enemy troops could be moved, billeted, or from which their attacks could be launched. Agent Orange was sprayed heavily by aircraft over huge swaths of the Southeast Asian landmass, infiltrating into the foliage, the ground water, the soil, and anything touched by the 133, ground or water. It was in the soil, in the foliage, on the ground, in the water, and dripped off the foliage onto our clothing as we patrolled in the bush. It came home with us, and to date has either directly or indirectly caused the deaths of thousands of Vietnam veterans.

In 1975, as the war in Vietnam was being abruptly ended, the US brought in thousands of Vietnamese fleeing communist persecution in their homeland. Many were brought to US military bases for housing, medical exams, and eventual movement into the country. One of these locations was Fort Indiantown Gap in Pennsylvania. I was offered the opportunity to visit and assist where possible with the resettlement of the thousands of Vietnamese who were now exiled from their own land. I helped locate family groups into base housing units, and even though my language skills were badly eroded, I was able to provide some language services to help American relief workers communicate with the often-confused refugees.

For many veterans, there have been opportunities to share our experiences with others in schools, churches and other social settings. These opportunities are seldom formally structured and have relied on the veteran's willingness to speak about his or her experiences to school classes, church and scouting groups, and other social organizations.

During my time as a member of Wisconsin's Vietnam Veterans Chapter 1, I was able to participate in the demonstration of a "tiger cage" device used to hold many captured Americans being held by the Viet Cong and the NVA. The device  was constructed from lengths of bamboo and barbed wire, configured into a large cube-like structure that was approximately seven feet long, four feet wide and three feet high. It was cramped! The cage was placed on the plaza of the Milwaukee War Memorial, and a different Vietnam veteran would spend a night in it each night for several weeks. I volunteered, was allowed an air mattress and an Army poncho liner and spent a very cramped night as a mock POW. It was a sobering experience. It was not even close to being the horror show experienced by our actual POW's but it's symbolism was unmistakable. The night I spent was punctuated by local Milwaukee police officers visiting to bring coffee. Vietnam didn't end for me simply because I came home. It has been ever-present in many forms for over five decades.

I still bear the scars of my battle wounds, often have recurrent nightmares about bad times, live with the results of my Agent Orange exposures and resulting conditions, and have worked for years to deal with the effects of Post-Traumatic Stress Disorder (PTSD). My generally successful life has been marred by the passings of men with whom I served both before and after my military service, some who became best friends and then lost to one or more serious medical conditions, many of which had their origins in the red laterite dirt/dust/mud/soil of Vietnam. Life goes on, and many of us have learned to live it one day at a time.

I offer a great deal of gratitude to those veterans who took their time and energy to assist me in my endeavor with this book. I am proud to share your stories with those who read *our* book, and which proceeds will go to the ongoing maintenance of the Vietnam Veterans Monument in Washington, DC.

In Dedication

This book is dedicated to my friends and fellow soldiers who did not survive their tours of duty:

Vernon Wilderspin
Haslett High School Class of 1961
Specialist 4, Combat Medic, 25th
Infantry Division
KIA - January 31, 1968

Raymond Suarez, Jr.
Lieutenant Colonel, Infantry
Province Senior Advisor
MACV Advisory Team 47 An Loc
Deputy Province Senior Advisor
MACV Advisory Team 67 Phuoc Long
(Song Be) KIA - February 29, 1969

John Edward Lynch
Specialist 4
Intelligence Specialist
PSYOP Air Crew Member
Company B 6th Psychological
Operations Group. KIA - June 15, 1969

In Dedication

I further offer dedication to several fellow Veteran Brothers who served in the Vietnam War, but who have passed since coming home. All were friends…a small few were "best" friends who I miss every day:

Richard Dean Hosier

John "Jack" O'Neil

Richard Dean Hosier

Donald DeNike

David W. Affleck

David K. H. Lee

Frank Coburn

About the Author

Chad Spawr served in the US Army from 1966 to 1973, including two tours in Vietnam. He served with the 1st Infantry Division, was a member of a MACV Advisory Team, and assigned to the 6th Psychological Operations Battalion/4th Psychological Operations Group, where he conducted Psychological Operations with the 1st Cavalry Division.

Following his military service, he completed undergraduate and graduate degrees at Michigan State University, the University of Michigan, and the Keller Graduate School of Management.

After a 39-year career in Labor-Management Relations and Human Resources Management, he retired and began writing and publishing books based on his military service.

Chad resides in Oakland County, Michigan with his lovely wife Linda, while their two sons, Alexander and Ryan, pursue their lives and careers.

Other Books By Chad Spawr

(Available through Amazon/Kindle E-Books and Paperback)

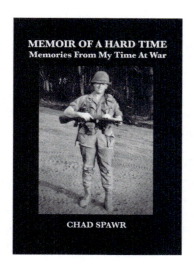

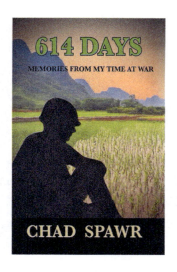

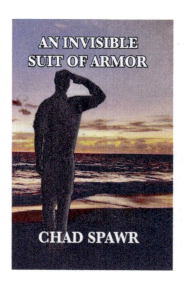

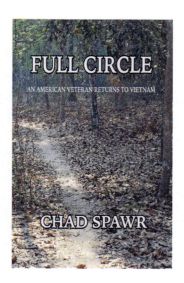

Printed by Amazon Italia Logistica S.r.l.
Torrazza Piemonte (TO), Italy

60838006R00090